ETHICS

That Guarantees and Accelerates Your Success

Victor Olewunne

Vista Press

Vista press
& Distribution Logistics Ltd.

ISBN: 9798856716312

Cover design by: Vista Advertising Ltd
Library of Congress Control Number: 2018675309
Printed in the United States of America

To my lovely wife, Ojiugo whose love and support I will always cherish.

CONTENTS

PROLOGUE

The Target Audience for this Book.

The target audience for this book with the title "Ethics: That Guarantees and Accelerates Your Success" includes a broad range of individuals who are interested in personal and professional development, ethical considerations, and achieving lasting success. Here are some specific groups that could find value in such a book:

Business Professionals and Entrepreneurs: Business leaders, managers, and entrepreneurs who want to understand how ethical principles can positively impact their organizations and contribute to sustainable success.

Students and Young Professionals: Aspiring professionals who are entering the workforce or pursuing higher education and are keen to build a foundation of ethical decision-making early in their careers.

Leaders and Managers: Individuals in leadership positions seeking insights on how to lead with integrity, create an ethical corporate culture, and drive team success through ethical leadership.

Ethics Enthusiasts: Those interested in philosophy, ethics, and morality who want to explore how ethical considerations intersect with real-world success, both personally and professionally.

Personal Development Seekers: Individuals looking to enhance their personal growth, character development, and overall well-being by integrating ethics into their life choices and actions.

Human Resources Professionals: HR practitioners who are responsible for promoting ethical behavior, managing organizational culture, and fostering ethical leadership within their companies.

Educators and Trainers: Teachers, trainers, and educators who aim to impart ethical values and decision-making skills to students, employees, or trainees.

Global Citizens: People who recognize the importance of ethical behavior on a global scale, including individuals interested in environmental sustainability, human rights, and social justice.

Professionals in Sensitive Fields: Individuals working in fields where ethical considerations are paramount, such as healthcare, law, journalism, and public service.

Civic and Community Leaders: Those involved in community leadership roles who want to learn how ethical principles can guide their efforts to create positive change.

People in Transition: Individuals undergoing personal or career transitions who are seeking guidance on how to approach new opportunities with ethical integrity.

General Readers: Anyone interested in exploring the connection between ethics and success, regardless of their specific background or profession.

The book's content is tailored to appeal to these various audiences, offering relevant examples, case studies, and actionable insights that resonate with their unique perspectives and goals.

INTRODUCTION

"Ethics is knowing the difference between what you have a right to do and what is right to do"- Potter Steward.

In a world fueled by ambition and aspiration, the pursuit of success often takes center stage. We are drawn to stories of remarkable achievement, captivated by the journeys of those who have triumphed against all odds. Yet, in the relentless pursuit of success, an essential facet often goes overlooked—the role of ethics.

Welcome to a journey that transcends traditional notions of success. This book, "Ethics: That Guarantees and Accelerates Your Success," beckons you to explore the profound interplay between ethical principles and the attainment of true, sustainable success. Beyond the ordinary realm of achievements and accolades lies a profound truth: success is not merely about reaching a destination; it's about how you get there.

In these pages, we delve into the heart of ethics and its transformative power. From the boardrooms of corporations to the chambers of personal growth, ethics emerges as the bedrock upon which extraordinary success is built. It is not merely a set of guidelines but a philosophy that shapes decisions, relationships, and the very essence of one's character.

Our exploration will navigate the intricate pathways of integrity, transparency, empathy, and responsibility. We will uncover the wisdom of ethical decision-making and the art of fostering authentic connections. We will learn how ethical leadership inspires collective growth and how the digital age challenges us to uphold moral values in new realms.

As you embark on this journey, be prepared to embark on a transformational voyage—a journey that challenges the conventional and empowers you to rise above the ordinary. Each chapter is a gateway to unlocking the secrets of ethical success, revealing the principles that not only guarantee but accelerate your ascent to greatness.

Through real-world examples, timeless philosophies, and actionable insights, you will discover that success achieved through ethics is not a mirage but a tangible reality. Whether you're a business leader aiming to steer your organization with purpose, an individual seeking personal growth with integrity, or an aspiring entrepreneur navigating uncharted waters, this book offers a guiding light.

Let us embark on this exploration with an open heart and a curious mind. Let us uncover the ways in which ethics becomes the compass that guides us toward our dreams, and the guiding star that ensures we reach the right destination—triumphant, fulfilled, and honorable.

The journey begins now, as we set sail on the seas of ethical success.

Setting the Stage: The Role of Ethics in Success

At the crossroads of ambition and achievement, a pivotal force often takes a backseat in discussions about success: ethics. In a world captivated by the allure of triumphs and breakthroughs, ethics stands as the unassuming yet undeniable cornerstone that shapes the very essence of genuine, lasting success.

This introduction serves as the prelude to our exploration— a journey that unveils the profound interconnection between ethics and success. Ethics, in its most fundamental sense, is the moral compass that guides our decisions and actions. It transcends mere legality and unveils the tapestry of integrity, honesty, and accountability that forms the foundation of meaningful achievements.

As the curtain rises on this discourse, it becomes evident that the story of success is incomplete without the role ethics plays. Ethics is not a superficial layer to be applied when convenient; it's a thread woven deeply into the fabric of every venture, relationship, and endeavor. It is the hidden force that separates fleeting success from the enduring kind, the difference between a house of cards and a monument of triumph.

We will embark on a journey through the landscapes of integrity, where consistency between actions and values paves the way for trust. This introduction lays the groundwork for understanding how ethics safeguards success, warding off the shadows of compromise and deceit that can tarnish even the most glittering achievements.

As we traverse these pages, we will navigate through the nuances of ethical choices and their far-reaching implications. From grand decisions that shape organizations to the seemingly small choices that mold personal character, ethics emerges as the compass that guides our way.

We will unravel the symbiotic relationship between ethics and long-term sustainability. In a world marked by rapid change and ever-evolving standards, ethics remains a constant, an anchor that ensures success does not merely fade away but blossoms into an enduring legacy.

As we dive into stories of leaders who have wielded ethics as their guiding light, you'll discover that true success isn't about shortcuts or underhanded tactics. Instead, it's about creating a symphony of achievement where every note resonates with authenticity, trust, and respect.

As the foundation of this exploration, this introduction reminds us that ethics is not a choice; it is an obligation, Immanuel Kant, the German philosopher calls it, a duty—a commitment to honor not just our aspirations but also the principles that govern them. It is a commitment to be remembered not only for what we accomplished but for how we achieved it.

Welcome to a journey that transcends the ordinary. The stage is set, the roles are defined, and the spotlight is on ethics —the understated protagonist that transforms success into a masterpiece of character, integrity, and lasting impact.

CHAPTER 1

The Foundation of Ethical Success

"A man's ethical behavior should be based effectually on sympathy, education, and social ties; no religious basis is necessary. Man would indeed be in a poor way if he had to be restrained by fear of punishment and hope of reward after death".

(Albert Einstein)

I n the intricate tapestry of success, ethical principles are the threads that weave lasting achievements into a masterpiece. The foundations of ethical success are not constructed overnight; they are meticulously carved from the bedrock of values, integrity, and responsibility.

Understanding Ethics: Definitions and Key Concepts

Ethics, often referred to as the moral compass of human conduct, encompasses a set of principles that guide individuals and organizations toward right actions and behaviors. At its core, ethics addresses questions of right and wrong, fairness and justice, and the responsibilities we hold toward ourselves and others.

This chapter unravels the definitions and key concepts that underpin ethical success. It illuminates the distinction between ethics and legality, emphasizing that adhering to the law is merely a starting point. True ethical success delves deeper, guided not just by legal boundaries but also by the broader principles of integrity, honesty, and compassion.

Definition

Ethics refers to the branch of philosophy that deals with questions of right and wrong, moral principles, and the principles that guide human behavior and decision-making. It encompasses the study of what is considered morally acceptable and unacceptable, as well as the reasoning behind these judgments. Ethics explores the values, virtues, and standards that individuals, societies, and organizations use to determine the appropriateness of actions and behaviors.

In a broader sense, ethics extends beyond philosophical inquiry and becomes a practical framework for making choices and conducting oneself in various contexts. Ethical considerations influence how people interact with others, how they approach challenges, and how they contribute to the betterment of society. Ethical principles often encompass concepts such as honesty, integrity, fairness, respect for others, and responsibility.

Ethics serves as a guide for individuals and groups to make informed decisions that align with their values, uphold moral principles, and contribute to the greater good. It plays a crucial role in shaping personal character, influencing professional conduct, and fostering a just and harmonious society.

Key Concepts

Ethics encompasses a range of key concepts that provide a framework for understanding and evaluating moral principles, values, and behaviors. Here are some fundamental key concepts of ethics:

Morality: Morality refers to the system of values, principles, and beliefs that guide human behavior and determine what is considered right and wrong within a particular context or society.

Moral Principles: These are foundational guidelines that help individuals and groups make ethical decisions. Examples include principles of honesty, fairness, justice, respect for autonomy, and beneficence (doing good).

Norms: Norms are established standards of behavior that are considered socially acceptable within a particular cultural or societal context. Ethical norms provide guidelines for appropriate conduct.

Values: Values are deeply held beliefs about what is important, meaningful, and worth pursuing. Ethical values influence personal and collective decision-making.

Virtues: Virtues are qualities or traits of character that are considered morally good and praiseworthy. Examples include honesty, courage, compassion, and integrity.

Duty and Obligation: Ethical theories often discuss the concept of duty or obligation, where individuals have a moral responsibility to fulfill certain duties or obligations toward others or society.

Consequences and Utility: Some ethical theories emphasize the consequences of actions, emphasizing the importance of maximizing overall well-being or utility. Utilitarianism, for example, evaluates actions based on their impact, that is, the greatest happiness for the greatest number of people.

Rights and Responsibilities: Ethical considerations often revolve around the concept of rights, which are entitlements individuals possess, and the corresponding responsibilities that come with respecting and upholding those rights.

Ethical Dilemmas: Ethical dilemmas arise when individuals or groups are faced with conflicting moral principles or choices, making it challenging to determine the right course of action.

Cultural Relativism: This concept acknowledges that ethical standards and practices can vary across cultures. Cultural relativism suggests that what is considered morally acceptable may differ based on cultural context.

Ethical Theories: These are systematic frameworks that provide guidance for ethical decision-making. Examples include deontological ethics with Immanuel Kant as its major proponent, virtue ethics which has Aristotle as its major proponent, utilitarianism with Jeremy Bentham as its major proponent, and ethical egoism with Ayn Rand and Max Stirner as its major proponents.

Integrity: Integrity refers to the consistency between one's actions, values, and principles. Acting with integrity means aligning behavior with ethical beliefs.

Ethical Leadership: Ethical leadership involves leading by example, demonstrating moral values, and promoting ethical behavior within organizations or communities.

Accountability: Accountability involves taking responsibility for one's actions and their consequences, especially when those actions affect others.

Ethical Reasoning: Ethical reasoning involves the process of evaluating ethical dilemmas and making decisions based on rational analysis, considering moral principles, a sense of duty, consequences, and other relevant factors.

These key concepts provide a foundation for exploring and discussing ethical issues, values, and principles across various contexts and situations. They offer a toolkit for individuals to engage in ethical reflection and decision-making.

The Link Between Ethics and Sustainable Success

While shortcuts and unethical practices might offer fleeting gains, they often sow the seeds of downfall. Sustainable success is built upon the foundation of ethical choices and actions. The decisions made today ripple through time, shaping the narrative of an individual's or organization's journey.

This chapter explores the symbiotic relationship between ethics and sustainable success. It delves into case studies that highlight how ethical failures have led to the downfall of once-mighty organizations, underscoring the importance of ethical considerations in the grand tapestry of achievement.

At the heart of it all lies the principle that ethical success isn't confined to immediate gains; it echoes through generations, becoming a legacy that enriches those who follow in its footsteps.

The Links

In the ever-evolving landscape of achievement, one undeniable truth emerges: true success is not a fleeting spark, but a flame that burns brightly across time. At the heart of this enduring triumph lies the profound link between ethics and sustainable success—a connection that goes beyond momentary gains to build a legacy that withstands the tests of time.

Integrity: The Keystone of Sustainable Success

Ethics infuses integrity into every facet of success. It transforms fleeting victories into lasting legacies by anchoring actions and decisions in principles that are unwavering and steadfast. The foundation of integrity is built on the bedrock of ethical principles—honesty, transparency, accountability—guiding individuals and organizations to stay true to their values, even in the face of challenges.

When integrity becomes the cornerstone of endeavors, trust flourishes. Stakeholders—be they customers, employees, partners, or communities—find solace in knowing that their interactions are governed by ethical conduct. Trust is the currency of sustainable success, a reservoir of goodwill that fuels enduring relationships and fosters growth.

Longevity Through Ethical Decision-Making

Ethical decision-making isn't merely a consideration; it's a compass that steers the journey toward sustainable success. Choices made through an ethical lens consider not only the immediate gains but also the long-term consequences. This focus on sustainable outcomes ensures that success doesn't wither away in the face of ethical shortcuts.

Ethical decisions often require resilience and patience, eschewing expedient paths for those that uphold values and principles. While the road may be longer, the destination is not just a destination—it's a foundation for continued growth, innovation, and prosperity.

Organizational Resilience and Reputation

Sustainable success extends its reach to organizational resilience. Ethical practices create a culture that adapts to challenges, bounces back from setbacks, and stands resilient against adversity. When ethics permeate an organization's DNA, it fosters a collective mindset that views challenges as opportunities for growth rather than roadblocks.

Moreover, ethical behavior safeguards an organization's most valuable asset: its reputation. A reputation built on ethical conduct serves as a shield against potential crises, fostering goodwill that can weather storms and bolster recovery. In a world of rapid information dissemination, the enduring value of an untarnished reputation cannot be overstated.

Legacy and Impact

At its essence, sustainable success is a legacy of impact—a testament to the positive influence one leaves behind. Ethical behavior amplifies this impact, resonating with stakeholders across generations. A legacy built on ethics goes beyond financial gains; it's a narrative that inspires, a story of principled dedication that encourages others to follow suit.

The link between ethics and sustainable success is not happenstance; it's a deliberate choice, a conscious commitment to shape success that endures, evolves, and extends its reach far beyond the immediate horizon. As we navigate the complex terrain of achievement, let ethics be the compass that guides us, ensuring that every step taken is a stride toward a brighter, more sustainable future.

Navigating Ethical Dilemmas with Integrity

In the labyrinth of life, ethical dilemmas are the crossroads that test the very essence of one's character. They challenge individuals to make choices that align with their values, even when the path ahead is uncertain or fraught with challenges and risk.

This equips you with the tools to navigate ethical dilemmas with grace and integrity. Through real-world scenarios and ethical decision-making frameworks, you'll learn how to assess options, weigh consequences, and choose the path that upholds both your aspirations and your principles.

The foundations of ethical success are not built on blind adherence to rules; they're forged through a deep understanding of values and a commitment to hold them steadfast even in the face of adversity. As we delve deeper into the heart of ethical success, you'll discover that these foundations are the compass that guides you toward achievement that resonates with authenticity, honor, and enduring impact.

Case Study

Enron Corporation: The Downfall of Ethical Integrity

Enron Corporation, once lauded as one of the largest and most innovative energy companies in the world, stands as a cautionary tale of how ethical issues can lead to a catastrophic downfall. The story of Enron's collapse serves as a stark reminder of the devastating consequences that arise when ethics are compromised in pursuit of short-term gains.

Background and Rise to Prominence

In the 1990s, Enron became a symbol of innovation and success in the energy industry. It embraced a model of trading energy contracts, pioneering the development of complex financial instruments. The company rapidly expanded its reach, generating massive revenues and garnering admiration from the financial community.

Ethical Breaches and Deceptive Practices

As Enron's reputation soared, internal ethical issues began to fester. Executives, driven by financial ambitions, engaged in unethical practices that aimed to artificially inflate the company's value. Among the most notorious tactics was the creation of special purpose entities (SPEs), which were used to hide debt and losses off the balance sheet. This deceptive accounting practice gave an illusion of profitability, even as the company's financial health deteriorated.

Lack of Transparency and Accountability

Enron's leadership promoted a culture of secrecy, where executives prioritized their personal financial gains over the interests of stakeholders. The company's auditors, Arthur Andersen, were implicated in overlooking and even participating in unethical practices, further eroding transparency and accountability.

The Catastrophic Collapse

By 2001, the unsustainable nature of Enron's financial house of cards became apparent. The company's stock price plummeted, and investors began to question its financial integrity. As investigations unfolded, the web of unethical practices was exposed, triggering a crisis of confidence that led to Enron's eventual bankruptcy in December 2001.

Consequences and Lessons

The fallout from Enron's collapse was severe. Thousands of employees lost their jobs, pensions, and savings. Shareholders faced massive financial losses. The scandal also led to the dissolution of Arthur Andersen, one of the "Big Five" accounting firms.

Enron's downfall serves as a glaring example of how ethical breaches can have far-reaching and devastating consequences. The company's disregard for integrity and transparency undermined its once-solid foundation, ultimately leading to its rapid demise. The Enron case highlights the importance of ethical leadership, accountability, and transparency in maintaining the trust of stakeholders and ensuring the sustainability of success.

Enron's legacy is a stark reminder that short-term gains achieved through unethical means are illusory and can lead to long-term irreparable damage to an organization's reputation, financial health, and impact on society at large.

CHAPTER 2

The Power of Integrity

"There's no way to succeed in business without the highest ethical standards"

- Jordon Belfort

Unveiling the Beacon of Ethical Leadership

I ntegrity, often regarded as the cornerstone of character, is a force that transcends time, circumstance, and success. It embodies the alignment of one's actions with their deeply held values and principles, reflecting an unwavering commitment to doing what is right, even when it's challenging or inconvenient. Within this steadfast commitment lies a power that can shape individuals, organizations, and entire societies.

A Pillar of Trust and Credibility

Integrity serves as the bedrock upon which trust and credibility are built. When individuals consistently demonstrate honesty and ethical behavior, they create a foundation of trust that others can rely upon. This foundation extends to relationships, institutions, and businesses. It forms the basis for healthy collaborations, strong partnerships, and enduring customer loyalty.

Consider a leader who upholds their promises, admits mistakes, and acts consistently with their stated values. Such a leader garners the respect and trust of their team, inspiring loyalty and dedication. This trust is not easily won but is a potent asset that paves the way for success in both personal and professional realms.

Influence and Ethical Leadership

Integrity and ethical leadership are inseparable companions. An ethical leader embodies integrity in their actions, decisions, and interactions. Their authenticity and moral compass become guiding lights that influence those around them. Ethical leaders inspire others to rise to higher standards, fostering a culture of accountability, transparency, and ethical behavior.

Imagine a CEO who prioritizes ethical considerations over short-term gains, leading their company with unwavering integrity. Their decisions ripple through the organization, shaping its ethical DNA. Employees are more likely to embrace these values, cultivating an environment that thrives on principled action and mutual respect.

Resilience in the Face of Challenges

Integrity becomes a beacon of light in times of adversity. When faced with difficult choices or ethical dilemmas, individuals with a strong sense of integrity remain resolute in their commitment to doing what is right. Their decisions are not swayed by external pressures or temptations; they are guided by an internal compass that always points towards ethical conduct.

Consider an entrepreneur who navigates ethical challenges by refusing to compromise on their values. Despite potential setbacks, they uphold their principles, demonstrating that success achieved through integrity is worth the temporary hardships. This resilience ultimately fortifies their character and the reputation of their endeavors.

A Lasting Legacy

The power of integrity extends beyond the present moment, leaving an indelible mark on history. Those who prioritize ethical behavior contribute to a legacy that endures. Whether as individuals or organizations, their impact is felt across generations, influencing future leaders and shaping the moral fabric of society.

Imagine an activist whose life is dedicated to fighting for justice and equality. Their unwavering commitment leaves a legacy that empowers others to carry the torch of change. This ripple effect, fueled by integrity, becomes a force for positive transformation that transcends time.

In a world often marked by complexity and ambiguity, integrity remains a guiding star—a constant amidst change, a touchstone of authenticity, and a force that propels individuals and societies toward greatness. It is the power of integrity that illuminates the path to a success that isn't merely measured by achievements but by the profound impact one has on the world.

The Core Principle: Integrity as the Bedrock of Success

In the symphony of human virtues, integrity stands as the melody that resonates with authenticity, honesty, and unwavering moral character. It is the core principle that underpins not only personal character but also the very foundation of success. Like a solid bedrock upon which magnificent structures are built, integrity serves as the unshakable foundation upon which lasting achievements are established.

Defining Integrity

Integrity is more than a word; it's a commitment to truthfulness, consistency, and ethical conduct. At its heart lies a deep alignment between words and actions, between stated values and lived principles. It's a pledge to be transparent and honorable in all endeavors, regardless of the circumstances.

Imagine an individual who consistently upholds their promises, speaks truthfully even when faced with challenges, and conducts themselves with honor. This individual's integrity becomes a guiding light, illuminating a path that others can trust and follow.

Trust: The Currency of Success

In the currency of success, trust is the most valuable asset. Integrity is the currency's minting press. When one's actions mirror their words and values, trust naturally emerges. Others can rely on the authenticity of their intentions and the dependability of their commitments.

Consider a leader who possesses unwavering integrity. Employees trust this leader's decisions because they know that every choice is guided by principles, not expediency. Trusting their leader, employees collaborate more effectively, leading to increased productivity, innovative thinking, and a harmonious work environment.

The Power of Reputation

Reputation is a reflection of integrity, and a positive reputation is a formidable ally in the pursuit of success. An individual or organization known for ethical behavior and consistent integrity enjoys the benefit of doubt and respect in the eyes of stakeholders.

Picture a business that is renowned for its ethical practices. Customers flock to its products, partners seek collaboration, and investors entrust their resources. The positive reputation earned through integrity becomes a magnet for success, attracting opportunities and fostering growth.

Integrity in Adversity

Integrity shines most brilliantly when adversity darkens the horizon. It's easy to make ethical choices when the path is smooth, but integrity reveals its true strength when challenges arise. An individual's commitment to doing what's right, even when it's difficult, speaks volumes about their character.

Imagine an athlete who, faced with the temptation to cheat, refuses to compromise their integrity. In doing so, they uphold the purity of their sport and their own self-respect. Their decision becomes a testament to the power of integrity to guide through storms and maintain one's moral compass.

A Lifelong Investment

Integrity is not a fleeting quality but a lifelong investment. It requires dedication to consistently make choices that align with ethical principles. The returns on this investment, however, are immeasurable: a life rich with respect, trust, meaningful relationships, and enduring success.

In the tapestry of success, integrity is the thread that binds achievements into a narrative of authenticity and impact. As we navigate the complexities of life, let integrity be our lodestar, reminding us that true success is not measured solely by what we accomplish, but by the legacy of honor and principled character we leave behind.

Navigating Ethical Dilemmas with Integrity

A Compass for Moral Clarity

Life is a journey of choices, and along the way, ethical dilemmas often emerge like crossroads, challenging us to navigate the path that aligns with our values. In these moments, integrity becomes the compass that guides us through the fog of uncertainty, illuminating the way forward with a steadfast commitment to what is right and just.

The Complexity of Ethical Dilemmas

Ethical dilemmas are not mere puzzles to solve; they are intricate scenarios where conflicting values collide. These dilemmas force us to confront difficult choices where each option carries its own set of moral implications. It is in these crossroads that our character is truly tested.

Imagine a doctor who faces the dilemma of disclosing a sensitive patient's medical information to their family. On one hand, there's the duty to respect patient confidentiality; on the other, the responsibility to ensure the patient's well-being. Navigating such dilemmas requires a delicate balance of ethical considerations.

The Role of Integrity

Integrity becomes our guiding North Star in the midst of ethical dilemmas. It is the unwavering commitment to upholding our principles, even when the options seem murky or the pressure is intense. Integrity compels us to make choices that align with our values, rather than taking the easy way out.

Consider a student who stumbles upon a test paper before the exam. While the allure of an easy A might be tempting, integrity reminds them that success achieved through dishonesty is hollow. Choosing to inform the teacher and face the consequences demonstrates a commitment to moral integrity.

Ethical Decision-Making Frameworks

Navigating ethical dilemmas often requires a systematic approach. Ethical decision-making frameworks, such as the utilitarian approach, deontological ethics, or virtue ethics, provide tools to analyze the situation from different angles, considering consequences, duties, and character traits.

Using these frameworks, an executive faced with a dilemma involving the potential layoff of employees may weigh the consequences of each option, considering both financial impact and ethical implications. This approach helps to make decisions that balance competing interests while maintaining integrity.

Transparency and Accountability

Integrity doesn't thrive in the shadows; it flourishes in the light of transparency and accountability. Sharing our thought processes and rationale behind our decisions not only invites others into our ethical journey but also helps us ensure that our choices align with our principles.

Imagine a leader who openly discusses the ethical dilemmas the organization faces, inviting input from team members. By fostering a culture of open dialogue, this leader ensures that decisions are made collectively, minimizing the risk of unethical choices going unchecked.

Growth Through Ethical Dilemmas

While ethical dilemmas pose challenges, they also offer opportunities for growth and self-discovery. Navigating these complexities tests our resolve, hones our critical thinking, and deepens our understanding of our values.

Consider an individual who grapples with a personal ethical dilemma involving a close friend's wrongdoing. Choosing to address the situation and have a difficult conversation, rather than ignoring it, leads to personal growth and a strengthened sense of integrity.

In the winding journey of life, ethical dilemmas are the threads that weave moral character into our stories. With integrity as our compass, we can navigate these dilemmas with clarity and conviction, emerging on the other side stronger, wiser, and resolute in our commitment to ethical principles.

Steps for navigating ethical dilemmas with integrity

Navigating ethical dilemmas with integrity requires thoughtful reflection, a commitment to ethical principles, and a systematic approach. Here are steps to help you navigate ethical dilemmas with integrity:

Identify and Define the Dilemma: Clearly understand the ethical dilemma you're facing. Define the conflicting values, interests, and potential consequences of each choice.

Clarify Your Values: Reflect on your personal values and principles. Consider what matters most to you and how your decisions align with these values.

Gather Information: Collect all relevant information related to the dilemma. Understand the context, implications, and potential outcomes of each decision.

Consider Different Perspectives: Think about how different stakeholders might be affected by your decision. Consider the perspectives of others involved, including colleagues, family, or those affected by your choices.

Use Ethical Frameworks: Utilize ethical decision-making frameworks to analyze the situation from different angles. Consider approaches like utilitarianism, deontology, virtue ethics, or ethical relativism to help you weigh the pros and cons of each option.

Evaluate Consequences: Consider the short-term and long-term consequences of each choice. Think about the potential impact on individuals, relationships, organizations, and society.

Seek Guidance: Consult mentors, advisors, or trusted friends who can offer different viewpoints and help you navigate the dilemma from an objective perspective.

Listen to Your Gut: Pay attention to your intuition. Often, a strong feeling about a particular choice indicates its alignment (or misalignment) with your values.

Choose the Least Harmful Option: Aim to make choices that minimize harm and promote the greatest good. Strive to find a solution that causes the least negative impact.

Transparency and Honesty: Be transparent with others about the ethical dilemma you're facing. Honesty demonstrates your commitment to ethical behavior and invites input from others.

Take Responsibility: Accept ownership of your decisions and their consequences. This demonstrates accountability and reflects your commitment to integrity.

Consider Long-Term Impact: Think about the long-term effects of your decision on your reputation, relationships, and personal growth.

Stay True to Your Principles: Prioritize your values over short-term gains. Even if a decision appears to be beneficial in the moment, it might erode your integrity over time.

Learn from the Experience: Reflect on the process and outcome. Consider how you might handle similar dilemmas in the future and how the experience has contributed to your personal growth.

Adapt and Adjust: Recognize that ethical dilemmas are complex, and there might not be a perfect solution. Be open to adjusting your approach as new information arises.

Remember that navigating ethical dilemmas with integrity is an ongoing practice. Each situation offers an opportunity to strengthen your ethical decision-making skills and reinforce your commitment to living by your values.

Real-Life Case: Lance Armstrong's Downfall

Background: Lance Armstrong was a celebrated American professional cyclist and a symbol of determination and success. However, his career and reputation came crashing down due to a lack of integrity surrounding his use of performance-enhancing drugs.

The Situation: Lance Armstrong won the prestigious Tour de France cycling race seven consecutive times from 1999 to 2005, making him a global icon and a source of inspiration for many. He also founded the Livestrong Foundation, which raised millions of dollars for cancer research and support.

Lack of Integrity: In 2012, the U.S. Anti-Doping Agency (USADA) conducted an investigation into allegations of doping by Armstrong and his cycling team. Despite his repeated denials, mounting evidence and testimonies from former teammates indicated that Armstrong had been using banned substances to enhance his performance for years.

Dramatic Fall from Grace: In 2013, Armstrong publicly admitted to using performance-enhancing drugs during his cycling career in an interview with Oprah Winfrey. His confession shattered his reputation and the image of a heroic survivor he had carefully cultivated. Armstrong was stripped of his seven Tour de France titles, banned from professional cycling for life, and faced legal and financial consequences.

Impact and Lessons: Lance Armstrong's downfall serves as a cautionary tale about the consequences of a lack of integrity, dishonesty, and the pursuit of success at any cost. His story highlights the importance of maintaining ethical standards, especially in the face of temptation or societal pressures.

Key Takeaways:

<u>Integrity Matters:</u> Armstrong's downfall demonstrates how lack of integrity can lead to irreparable damage to one's reputation and legacy.

<u>Ethical Shortcuts Have Consequences:</u> His story underscores the dangers of taking unethical shortcuts, even if they appear to lead to short-term success.

<u>Transparency and Accountability:</u> Being honest and accountable for one's actions, even in the face of immense pressure, is essential to maintaining trust and credibility.

Lance Armstrong's case serves as a powerful example of how a lack of integrity can lead to a spectacular downfall, illustrating the importance of ethical behavior, accountability, and the long-term consequences of dishonesty.

CHAPTER 3

Building Authentic Relationships

"Disciplining yourself to do
what you know is right
and important, although difficult,
is the highroad to pride, self-esteem,
and personal satisfaction."

- Margaret Thatcher

The Art of Genuine Connection

In a world driven by digital interactions and fleeting connections, the value of authentic relationships shines brighter than ever. Building authentic relationships is not merely about amassing contacts; it's about fostering genuine connections that enrich our lives, personally and professionally. It is a journey that transcends superficiality, delving into the depths of human connection and understanding.

The Foundations of Authenticity

Authentic relationships are built on a foundation of honesty, transparency, and mutual respect. Authenticity requires being true to yourself and allowing others to see you for who you genuinely are. It is about sharing your thoughts, feelings, and experiences without pretense or facade.

Imagine meeting someone who engages in conversations with genuine interest, expresses vulnerability, and actively listens. Their authenticity creates a safe space that encourages openness and connection, setting the stage for a meaningful relationship.

Effective Communication and Active Listening

Central to building authentic relationships is effective communication. This involves not only expressing yourself clearly but also actively listening to others. Authentic connections are nurtured when people feel heard, understood, and valued.

Consider a situation where two individuals engage in a conversation where both speak and listen attentively. Through this exchange, they learn about each other's perspectives, aspirations, and experiences, fostering a bond that goes beyond surface-level interactions.

Empathy and Understanding

Empathy is the cornerstone of authentic relationships. It is the ability to put yourself in someone else's shoes, to understand their emotions and experiences. Empathy fosters a deep connection, as it shows that you genuinely care about another person's feelings and well-being.

Imagine a friend who supports you during difficult times, offering a listening ear and a shoulder to lean on. Their empathy creates a bond of trust and understanding that forms the essence of an authentic friendship.

Shared Values and Common Ground

Authentic relationships often find common ground in shared values, interests, or goals. These commonalities provide a strong foundation for connection and create a sense of belonging.

Consider a team of colleagues who are passionate about a shared project or cause. Their alignment around a common goal not only drives their collaboration but also forms the basis for a genuine camaraderie that extends beyond the workplace.

Consistency and Reliability

Authentic relationships are built on consistency and reliability. Being there for someone consistently, offering support, and honoring commitments build trust over time.

Imagine a mentor who consistently provides guidance and advice, helping you navigate challenges. Their reliability and willingness to invest time in your growth create a bond of trust and appreciation.

Investing Time and Effort

Building authentic relationships requires investment. It takes time, effort, and a genuine interest in getting to know others on a deeper level. Authentic connections aren't forged overnight; they evolve through shared experiences and meaningful interactions.

Consider a family that gathers regularly for meals and conversations. Their commitment to spending time together strengthens the familial bond, creating lasting memories and a sense of belonging.

In a world of fleeting interactions and social media distractions, authentic relationships stand as beacons of connection and belonging. They offer a refuge from the shallow and the transient, providing a space where we can be truly ourselves and find meaningful companionship. As you embark on the journey of building authentic relationships, remember that the effort you invest will yield immeasurable rewards of genuine connection, understanding, and shared experiences.

Ethical Networking: Creating Genuine Connection

Networking, often seen as a means to an end, has the potential to transcend transactional exchanges and evolve into something deeper and more meaningful: ethical networking. This approach centers on building connections that are rooted in authenticity, honesty, and mutual respect. Ethical networking shifts the focus from "what can I gain?" to "how can we mutually benefit and learn from each other?" It's a journey towards forging relationships that enrich both personal and professional lives.

Authenticity as the Keystone

At the heart of ethical networking lies authenticity. Being genuine and true to oneself in interactions forms the foundation of meaningful connections. Authentic networking involves sharing your true self, aspirations, and challenges, rather than projecting a polished image.

Imagine attending a networking event where individuals share their genuine experiences and engage in real conversations. These interactions create an environment of trust and camaraderie, fostering connections that extend beyond the event.

Mutual Respect and Reciprocity

Ethical networking thrives on mutual respect and reciprocity. It is about valuing each person's expertise, perspectives, and contributions. Instead of focusing solely on personal gain, ethical networking involves seeking ways to contribute to the success and growth of others.

Consider a scenario where professionals collaborate on projects by leveraging their respective strengths. This mutually beneficial partnership exemplifies ethical networking, where each party contributes to the collective success.

Active Listening and Empathy

Ethical networking requires active listening and empathy. By genuinely understanding others' viewpoints, challenges, and goals, you can establish connections that go beyond surface-level interactions.

Imagine engaging in a conversation where you listen intently, ask thoughtful questions, and demonstrate genuine interest in the other person's journey. This practice of empathy nurtures connections based on understanding and shared experiences.

Transparency and Openness

Transparency is a cornerstone of ethical networking. Being open about your goals, limitations, and intentions fosters trust and credibility. It allows for informed decision-making when establishing connections.

Consider disclosing your objectives and expectations when reaching out to potential connections. This transparency sets the tone for an honest and fruitful relationship, built on shared understanding.

Long-Term Relationship Building

Ethical networking is not confined to immediate gains; it is about building relationships for the long term. Cultivating connections over time allows for the organic growth of genuine rapport and trust.

Imagine consistently engaging with a network of professionals, sharing insights, celebrating successes, and offering support during challenges. This sustained investment in relationships exemplifies ethical networking's focus on enduring connections.

Supporting Growth and Learning

Ethical networking is a platform for growth and learning. By connecting with diverse individuals, you expose yourself to different perspectives, experiences, and opportunities for personal and professional development.

Consider joining a network where members actively mentor and guide each other. This collaborative approach fosters an environment of growth, where ethical networking becomes a catalyst for continuous learning.

Ethical networking transcends superficial interactions to create a tapestry of authentic connections. By valuing authenticity, mutual respect, and reciprocity, ethical networking transforms the way we build relationships, enriching our lives with meaningful connections that contribute to both our personal and professional well-being.

Trust and Collaboration: Keys to Accelerated Growth

In the dynamic landscape of today's interconnected world, growth isn't solely about individual achievements; it's about the power of collective progress. Two pivotal factors that drive this collective advancement are trust and collaboration. When harnessed effectively, trust and collaboration act as accelerators, propelling individuals, teams, and organizations toward accelerated growth and shared success.

The Foundation of Trust

Trust is the invisible thread that weaves together relationships, creating bonds that are resilient, enduring, and rooted in confidence. It is the belief that others will act in your best interest and uphold their commitments. Trust lubricates the wheels of interaction, enabling seamless collaboration and fruitful partnerships.

Imagine a team where members trust each other's expertise, intentions, and follow-through. This trust transforms interactions from cautious exchanges into a free-flowing exchange of ideas, creativity, and innovation.

Cultivating Trust through Integrity

Trust is not simply granted; it is earned. It is built through consistent actions that demonstrate integrity, reliability, and authenticity. When individuals keep their promises, act transparently, and prioritize ethical behavior, trust naturally blossoms.

Consider a leader who models unwavering integrity, consistently making decisions aligned with ethical principles. Their actions build a culture of trust within the team, fostering an environment where growth and collaboration flourish.

The Synergy of Collaboration

Collaboration goes beyond mere cooperation; it is the fusion of diverse perspectives, skills, and talents to create something greater than the sum of its parts. Collaborative efforts leverage collective strengths, leading to innovative solutions, efficient problem-solving, and holistic growth.

Imagine a cross-functional team working on a project, each member bringing their unique expertise to the table. Through collaboration, the team transcends individual limitations, uncovering novel strategies and accelerating progress.

Breaking Down Silos through Collaboration

Collaboration erases the boundaries of silos and departments, fostering a culture of interconnectedness. When individuals collaborate across disciplines, they gain fresh insights, learn new approaches, and infuse their work with diverse perspectives.

Consider an organization that encourages employees to participate in cross-departmental projects. This collaborative environment sparks creativity and cultivates a shared sense of purpose, driving the organization's growth and innovation.

Trust as the Catalyst for Collaboration

Trust and collaboration are intrinsically linked. A foundation of trust is the fuel that powers effective collaboration. When individuals trust each other, they're more likely to share ideas openly, take calculated risks, and work harmoniously toward common goals.

Imagine a group of entrepreneurs entering into a collaborative partnership to launch a new venture. Their trust in each other's abilities and intentions ignites a synergy that fuels their collective efforts, accelerating the growth of their startup.

A Virtuous Cycle of Growth

Trust and collaboration create a virtuous cycle: as trust deepens, collaboration flourishes; as collaboration flourishes, trust strengthens further. This cycle propels individuals and organizations toward accelerated growth, innovation, and success.

Picture a network of professionals who trust each other's expertise and willingly collaborate on projects. The resulting collective expertise transforms challenges into opportunities and propels their individual and collective growth.

In the intricate dance of growth, trust and collaboration are the partners that lead the waltz. They harmonize effort, amplify impact, and propel individuals and organizations toward accelerated achievements. As we navigate the complexities of our interconnected world, embracing trust and collaboration becomes not just a strategy but a philosophy that cultivates a culture of accelerated growth and shared success.

Case Study: Authentic Relationship Building in the Nonprofit Sector

Background: The charity organization "Global Hope Foundation" is dedicated to providing education and healthcare resources to underserved communities in developing countries. One of its key team members, Emily Williams, exemplified the power of authenticity in relationship building within the nonprofit sector.

The Situation: Emily, with a background in public health, joined Global Hope Foundation as a project coordinator. She recognized that authentic relationships were vital not only for fundraising but also for creating sustainable impact on the ground. She understood that building trust with local communities was essential for successful project implementation.

Building Authentic Connections: Instead of just focusing on donor relations, Emily took the time to connect with the communities she worked with. She immersed herself in their cultures, learned their languages, and truly listened to their needs and concerns. She didn't approach them with a predetermined agenda; instead, she worked collaboratively to understand their priorities and how the organization could support them.

During one project in a rural village, Emily spent weeks living with the community, working alongside them, and genuinely engaging in their daily lives. She earned their trust and respect by showing her commitment to their well-being beyond the scope of her role.

Nurturing Trust and Empathy: Emily's dedication to authenticity paid off. The community began to see her not just as a representative of an organization, but as a friend and ally. This trust enabled open and honest communication, which was critical for identifying the most effective ways to address their needs.

When challenges arose, such as delays in project funding, Emily communicated transparently with the community. Instead of hiding the difficulties, she discussed the situation openly and worked with the community to find alternative solutions. This approach reinforced the sense that they were partners working together towards a common goal.

The Impact: Emily's authenticity had a profound impact on the organization's projects. The community's active involvement and ownership led to successful implementation, with projects tailored to their specific needs. Additionally, the community became advocates for Global Hope Foundation's work, spreading the word about the organization's positive impact.

Beyond the immediate projects, Emily's authentic relationships paved the way for lasting partnerships. The organization gained a reputation for its respectful and community-centered approach, attracting more support and partnerships over time.

Key Takeaways:

Cultural Understanding: Authentic relationship building requires a genuine understanding of the cultural context and values of the community.

Listening and Collaboration: Actively listening and collaborating with the community fosters trust and shared ownership.

Transparency: Open and transparent communication, even in challenging situations, reinforces trust and empathy.
Long-Term Impact: Authentic relationships lead to sustainable impact, partnerships, and advocacy.

Emily's case demonstrates that authenticity is not just a personal quality but a strategic approach that can transform relationships and drive meaningful change. Her commitment to building genuine connections resulted in empowered communities, successful projects, and a stronger reputation for Global Hope Foundation within the nonprofit sector.

CHAPTER 4

Leading with Ethics

"True leadership is moral authority, not formal authority. Leadership is a choice, not a position. The choice is to follow universal timeless principles, which will build trust and respect from the entire organization. Those with formal authority alone will lose this trust and respect."

- Steven Covey

Guiding the Journey with Integrity

L eadership is not just about charting a course to success; it is about setting the moral compass that guides individuals, teams, and organizations on their journey. Leading with ethics is not a mere choice; it is a responsibility to uphold principles that foster trust, integrity, and sustainable success. It is a commitment to be a beacon of ethical behavior that illuminates the path for others to follow.

Ethics as the North Star

At the heart of leading with ethics lies the unwavering commitment to ethical principles. It's about aligning decisions, actions, and behaviors with values that prioritize honesty, fairness, respect, and social responsibility. Ethical leaders recognize that their choices set the tone for the entire organization's culture and reputation.

Imagine a CEO who consistently makes decisions that reflect the organization's values, even in the face of challenging situations. Their ethical leadership establishes a culture where employees, partners, and stakeholders trust in the organization's integrity.

Modeling Integrity

Leading with ethics begins with leading by example. Ethical leaders embody the values they espouse, demonstrating integrity through their actions and decisions. Their behavior becomes a model for others to emulate, fostering a culture of authenticity and accountability.

Consider a manager who admits mistakes, takes ownership of failures, and treats everyone with respect. Their humility and authenticity inspire employees to mirror these behaviors, contributing to a workplace culture built on integrity.

Ethical Decision-Making

Ethical leaders approach decision-making with a conscious consideration of the ethical implications. They seek to balance short-term gains with long-term consequences, striving to make choices that align with their values and the organization's mission.

Imagine a leader faced with a decision that could yield immediate financial gains but compromise the organization's long-term reputation. By prioritizing ethical considerations, they choose the path that upholds their values and preserves trust.

Transparency and Open Communication

Ethical leaders embrace transparency and open communication.

They provide clear explanations for their decisions and encourage open dialogue within the organization. This practice not only builds trust but also fosters an environment where concerns can be raised without fear of retribution.

Consider a team leader who shares the reasoning behind strategic shifts, including potential challenges. Their transparent communication empowers team members with a holistic understanding, fostering a sense of ownership and commitment.

Balancing Stakeholder Interests

Leading with ethics requires balancing the interests of various stakeholders—employees, customers, shareholders, and the broader society. Ethical leaders consider the needs and perspectives of all parties, aiming to create outcomes that benefit everyone involved.

Imagine a community leader who navigates complex decisions by considering the well-being of residents, local businesses, and the environment. Their commitment to balancing stakeholder interests fosters harmony and sustainability.

Inspiring a Legacy of Integrity

Leading with ethics extends beyond the present moment; it is about inspiring a legacy of ethical behavior. Ethical leaders leave a mark that influences future leaders and shapes the organization's culture for years to come.

Picture an educator who instills ethical values in their students through mentorship and guidance. These students, as they step into leadership roles, carry forward the legacy of integrity, creating a ripple effect of positive influence.

In the tapestry of leadership, leading with ethics weaves threads of authenticity, accountability, and moral courage. It's a commitment to charting a course that not only achieves success but also leaves a lasting impact of trust, responsibility, and integrity. As leaders navigate the complexities of their roles, let ethics be the guiding star that illuminates the path toward a brighter, more ethical future.

Ethical Leadership: Inspiring Teams for Collective Success

Ethical leadership is not just a style; it is a mindset that shapes the very fabric of an organization. It is about leading by example, fostering a culture of trust, and empowering individuals to achieve their best while upholding the highest standards of ethics. Ethical leaders don't just focus on individual accomplishments; they inspire teams to work collaboratively, contributing to a shared success that goes beyond the bottom line.

Setting the Ethical Tone

Ethical leaders set the tone for the organization by consistently demonstrating integrity, transparency, and accountability. They walk the talk, making decisions that align with the organization's values and inspiring others to do the same.

Imagine a leader who addresses challenges head-on, admitting mistakes and taking responsibility for the outcomes. Their actions create an environment where honesty and integrity are valued, laying the foundation for a culture of ethical behavior.

Fostering a Culture of Trust

Ethical leadership builds trust—trust between leaders and team members, and trust within teams themselves. When individuals believe that their leaders are genuinely committed to ethical behavior, they're more likely to trust their decisions and collaborate effectively.

Consider a team where the leader encourages open dialogue

and respects diverse viewpoints. This leader's commitment to fostering a culture of trust enables team members to express themselves freely, leading to enhanced collaboration and innovative solutions.

Empowering Through Ethics

Ethical leaders empower their teams by entrusting them with responsibility and autonomy. When individuals are given the freedom to make decisions aligned with ethical principles, they feel valued and motivated to contribute their best efforts.

Imagine a manager who delegates tasks based on team members' strengths and encourages them to make decisions independently. This empowerment not only increases job satisfaction but also fosters a sense of ownership and commitment to ethical outcomes.

Navigating Ethical Challenges Together

Ethical leaders acknowledge that ethical challenges are part of the leadership journey. Instead of avoiding these challenges, they engage their teams in ethical discussions, allowing for diverse perspectives and solutions to emerge.

Consider a leader who involves their team in ethical decision-making, seeking input and collaborating on solutions. By engaging in open conversations, the team gains a deeper understanding of ethical considerations and feels invested in the outcomes.

Cultivating Ethical Role Models

Ethical leaders understand that their influence extends beyond their own actions. They cultivate ethical role models within their teams, nurturing a collective commitment to ethical behavior and inspiring future leaders.

Picture a leader who mentors junior team members, guiding

them through ethical dilemmas and helping them make principled decisions. These mentees, as they grow in their roles, carry forward the values of ethical leadership, contributing to a culture of integrity.

Measuring Success Beyond Profit

Ethical leadership recognizes that success isn't solely measured by financial gains. It encompasses factors like employee satisfaction, community impact, and sustainable practices. Ethical leaders consider the holistic impact of their decisions on stakeholders and society.

Imagine a CEO who champions corporate social responsibility initiatives that positively impact the local community. Their commitment to ethical leadership goes beyond profits, aligning the organization's success with positive societal outcomes.

Ethical leadership goes beyond individual achievements; it's about creating an environment where individuals are empowered to collaborate, innovate, and excel while upholding ethical principles. By setting the ethical tone, fostering trust, and inspiring collective success, ethical leaders create a legacy of integrity, collaboration, and lasting impact.

Balancing Empathy and Accountability in Leadership: The Art of Harmonious Guidance

Leadership is a delicate balance between fostering a supportive, empathetic environment and maintaining a sense of accountability and responsibility. Striking this equilibrium is crucial for creating a culture that values both the well-being of individuals and the achievement of collective goals. Successful leaders understand that empathy and accountability are not opposing forces; rather, they are complementary elements that, when balanced, lead to a harmonious and effective leadership approach.

The Power of Empathy

Empathy is the cornerstone of meaningful leadership. It is the ability to understand and share the feelings of others, cultivating a sense of connection, trust, and mutual respect. Empathetic leaders create an atmosphere where individuals feel heard, valued, and understood.

Imagine a leader who takes the time to listen to their team members' concerns, acknowledges their struggles, and offers support when needed. This leader's empathetic approach fosters a positive work environment where individuals feel emotionally supported.

Creating a Supportive Environment

Empathetic leaders prioritize creating an environment that supports the well-being of their team members. They recognize that individuals are not just employees; they are people with personal lives, challenges, and aspirations. This awareness informs their approach to management.

Consider a manager who encourages work-life balance, offers flexible scheduling, and provides resources for mental and emotional well-being. This leader's efforts contribute to a culture that values holistic health and happiness.

Promoting Open Communication

Empathy paves the way for open communication. When team members feel that their thoughts and feelings are valued, they're more likely to share their ideas, concerns, and feedback. This open dialogue enhances collaboration and leads to more informed decision-making.

Imagine a team where the leader encourages open discussions about challenges and setbacks. By valuing input from all members and addressing concerns, this leader fosters a sense of psychological safety, enabling team members to express themselves freely.

The Importance of Accountability

Accountability is the other side of the leadership coin. It's about holding oneself and others responsible for meeting expectations, fulfilling commitments, and achieving goals. Leaders who emphasize accountability create a culture of discipline and reliability.

Consider a leader who sets clear performance expectations, tracks progress, and holds team members responsible for their contributions. This leader's commitment to accountability ensures that tasks are completed efficiently and that the team works cohesively toward its objectives.

Striking the Balance

Balancing empathy and accountability requires finesse. It involves recognizing that holding individuals accountable can be done with empathy and understanding, and that empathy doesn't mean excusing lack of responsibility. Successful leaders find ways to merge these two aspects to create a well-rounded leadership approach.

Imagine a leader who provides constructive feedback in a supportive manner, highlighting areas for improvement while offering guidance for growth. This leader's balanced approach encourages personal development while maintaining accountability.

Fostering Growth Through Balance

Leaders who strike the balance between empathy and accountability foster an environment of growth. They empower individuals to take ownership of their responsibilities while providing the support needed for their success.

Picture a team where the leader promotes accountability by setting challenging goals, while also offering mentorship, resources, and encouragement. This approach inspires team members to stretch their capabilities and achieve their potential.

In the tapestry of leadership, empathy and accountability are woven together to create a culture of understanding, responsibility, and growth. Balancing these elements requires sensitivity, wisdom, and adaptability, but the result is a leadership style that nurtures both individuals and collective success.

Case Study: Leading With Ethics in the Automotive Industry

Background: Carlos Mendez was appointed as the CEO of "GreenDrive Motors," a well-established automotive company known for its commitment to sustainability and innovative technology. Carlos was a firm believer in leading with ethics and saw his role as an opportunity to drive positive change in the industry.

The Situation: When Carlos took the helm, he recognized that the automotive industry was facing increasing pressure to address environmental concerns and adopt sustainable practices. He understood that leading with ethics was not only a matter of compliance but also a strategic choice that could enhance the company's reputation and long-term viability.

Ethical Decision-Making: Carlos initiated a series of ethical changes within GreenDrive Motors. He committed to reducing the company's carbon footprint by investing in electric and hybrid vehicle technologies. He also established clear guidelines for responsible sourcing of materials, ensuring that the supply chain adhered to fair labor practices and environmental standards.

One key decision was to invest in research and development to create vehicles with lower emissions, as well as exploring alternative energy sources for manufacturing processes. Carlos understood that these changes might involve initial costs, but he believed that the long-term benefits would outweigh the challenges.

Building an Ethical Culture: Carlos understood that leading with ethics required a cultural shift within the organization. He focused on fostering a work environment where employees felt empowered to voice concerns and suggest ethical improvements. He promoted transparency and accountability at all levels, emphasizing that ethical behavior was everyone's responsibility.

He also implemented training programs that educated employees about the company's ethical values and their role in upholding them. This helped align the entire workforce with the company's ethical vision.

The Impact: Carlos's commitment to leading with ethics had a transformative impact on GreenDrive Motors. The company's reputation improved significantly, attracting environmentally conscious consumers and investors. The focus on sustainability and ethical practices also set GreenDrive Motors apart from competitors, making it a leader in the industry.

Financially, the company's investments in sustainable technologies led to increased market share as demand for eco-friendly vehicles grew. GreenDrive Motors' commitment to ethical leadership also helped attract top talent who aligned with the company's values.

Key Takeaways:

Strategic Ethical Leadership: Leading with ethics involves making deliberate decisions that align with ethical values and long-term goals.

Cultural Transformation: Building an ethical culture requires fostering transparency, accountability, and empowerment among employees.

Long-Term Benefits: Ethical leadership can lead to improved reputation, increased market share, and a competitive advantage. Balancing Profit and Ethics: Ethical decisions may involve short-term costs but can yield long-term financial and reputational benefits.

Carlos Mendez's case exemplifies how ethical leadership can

drive positive change within an industry. By aligning the company's values with sustainable practices, he not only improved GreenDrive Motors' bottom line but also contributed to the larger goal of addressing environmental concerns and advancing ethical standards in the automotive sector.

CHAPTER 5

Ethical Decision-Making

*"The right way is not always
the popular and easy way.
Standing for right when it is
unpopular is a true test of
moral character."*

- Margaret Chase Smith

Navigating the Moral Landscape

Every day, individuals and leaders are faced with choices that have ethical implications. Ethical decision-making is the process of evaluating these choices through the lens of moral principles, values, and standards. It's about making choices that align with one's integrity, uphold ethical principles, and consider the impact on individuals, communities, and society at large.

The Complexity of Ethical Dilemmas

Ethical decision-making often involves navigating complex dilemmas where different values or principles come into conflict. These dilemmas require individuals to weigh the pros and cons of each option, considering the ethical implications and potential consequences.

Imagine a manager who must decide between maximizing short-term profits or prioritizing the well-being of employees. This ethical dilemma requires careful consideration of the long-term impact on both financial stability and employee morale.

The Role of Ethical Frameworks

Ethical decision-making can be guided by various ethical frameworks, each offering a structured approach to analyzing dilemmas. Frameworks like utilitarianism, deontology, virtue ethics, and ethical relativism provide tools to evaluate choices based on principles such as consequences, duties, virtues, or cultural context.

Consider an individual using the utilitarian approach to decide between two options, considering which choice would lead to the greatest overall happiness and well-being for all involved parties.

Consideration of Stakeholders

Ethical decision-making extends beyond personal values to consider the interests of stakeholders. Individuals must think about how their choices affect employees, customers, shareholders, and the broader community. This perspective helps balance individual interests with the greater good.

Imagine a business leader deciding whether to invest in environmentally sustainable practices. Ethical decision-making involves evaluating the impact on not only the company's profitability but also the environment and the local community.

Transparency and Accountability

Ethical decision-making is enhanced by transparency and accountability. Openly discussing the ethical considerations behind decisions fosters a culture of trust and encourages collaboration. Individuals who take responsibility for their choices demonstrate their commitment to ethical behavior.

Consider a leader who openly shares the ethical challenges the team is facing and invites input from team members. This transparent approach encourages a collective effort to navigate ethical dilemmas.

Long-Term Consequences

Ethical decision-making takes into account not only immediate outcomes but also the long-term consequences of choices. Consideration of how decisions affect an individual's reputation, relationships, and personal growth contributes to a more holistic perspective.

Imagine a professional who chooses to prioritize ethical behavior in a highly competitive industry. While this choice might involve short-term sacrifices, the long-term benefits include a strong reputation, trust from clients, and sustained success.

The Ethical Legacy

Ethical decision-making leaves a lasting impact on an individual's character and reputation. It contributes to building a legacy of integrity, responsible behavior, and trustworthiness. As individuals consistently make ethical choices, they contribute to the broader societal fabric of ethics and values.

Picture a leader who consistently makes decisions based on ethical principles, inspiring their team to do the same. This leader's ethical legacy creates a culture where ethics are valued, and individuals are empowered to make principled choices.

Ethical decision-making is the compass that guides individuals through the complexities of life's choices. By considering moral principles, stakeholders' interests, and long-term consequences, individuals navigate the moral landscape with integrity and contribute to a world shaped by responsible behavior and ethical considerations.

The Decision Crossroads: Approaches to Ethical Decision-Making

Ethical decision-making often resembles a crossroads where individuals must navigate through the intricacies of conflicting values, principles, and interests. At this juncture, having a well-defined approach to ethical decision-making provides a roadmap to navigate these complexities and arrive at choices that align with one's integrity and ethical compass. Here, we explore several common approaches that individuals can employ when faced with ethical dilemmas.

Utilitarianism: The Pursuit of the Greater Good

Utilitarianism is an ethical approach that prioritizes the greatest overall happiness or well-being for the greatest number of people. When using the utilitarian approach, individuals evaluate the consequences of each choice and opt for the option that maximizes positive outcomes while minimizing negative ones.

Imagine a leader deciding whether to allocate company resources to a project that benefits a larger segment of the workforce, even if it means disappointing a few employees. The utilitarian approach would likely guide them to choose the option that benefits the majority.

Deontology: Duty and Moral Rules

Deontology emphasizes the importance of moral rules and duties. Individuals who use this approach focus on the inherent rightness or wrongness of actions, regardless of their consequences. Decisions are based on principles that uphold ethical standards, irrespective of the outcomes they might produce.

Consider a healthcare professional who faces the dilemma of disclosing a patient's confidential medical information. Despite potential negative consequences, they choose to uphold their duty to protect patient confidentiality, as guided by ethical principles.

Virtue Ethics: Cultivating Moral Character

Virtue ethics centers on the development of moral character. Individuals who embrace this approach prioritize qualities like honesty, courage, and compassion. Decisions are guided by an assessment of how a choice reflects and enhances one's moral virtues.

Imagine an entrepreneur deciding whether to prioritize profits over environmental sustainability. A leader who values virtues like responsibility and sustainability might choose to invest in eco-friendly practices, even if it entails short-term financial sacrifices.

Ethical Relativism: Cultural and Contextual Considerations

Ethical relativism acknowledges that ethical values can vary across cultures and contexts. This approach suggests that the right course of action may differ based on cultural norms and circumstances. Individuals using this approach consider the values and expectations of the specific context in which they are making a decision.

Consider a diplomat negotiating a sensitive international agreement. Ethical relativism would encourage them to consider the cultural norms and values of both negotiating parties, adapting their approach to align with the context.

Principlism: Integrating Multiple Principles

Principlism involves integrating multiple ethical principles to guide decision-making. Individuals using this approach weigh the competing principles involved in a dilemma and aim to find a balance that respects all relevant values.

Imagine a professional grappling with the decision of whether to report a colleague's unethical behavior. Principlism would encourage considering principles like honesty, loyalty, and accountability to arrive at a decision that balances these competing values.

Reflective Judgment: Engaging Critical Thinking

Reflective judgment involves critical thinking and assessment of the complexity of ethical dilemmas. Individuals using this approach gather information, analyze potential outcomes, and consider the perspectives of various stakeholders before making a decision.

Consider a manager faced with a decision that impacts employees and shareholders. Reflective judgment would involve analyzing the potential consequences for both parties, evaluating the ethical implications, and considering alternative solutions.

In the realm of ethical decision-making, the approaches described above provide individuals with tools to navigate the crossroads of complex dilemmas. By considering factors like consequences, duties, virtues, context, and principles, individuals can make informed choices that reflect their values, uphold ethical standards, and contribute to a more responsible and ethical society.

Strategies to Overcome Ethical Challenges: Navigating the Moral Maze

Ethical challenges are an inherent part of life, often requiring individuals to make difficult decisions that align with their values and principles. Overcoming these challenges demands a blend of self-awareness, critical thinking, and moral courage.

Here are strategies to help individuals navigate the ethical maze and make principled choices when faced with dilemmas.

1. Self-Reflection and Awareness: Begin by understanding your own values, beliefs, and ethical principles. Reflect on what matters most to you and how your decisions align with these core aspects. Cultivating self-awareness enables you to make decisions that are congruent with your personal ethics.

2. Seek Guidance and Advice: Reach out to mentors, colleagues, friends, or professionals you trust when confronted with ethical challenges. Their insights and different perspectives can offer clarity and guidance, helping you view the situation from various angles.

3. Utilize Ethical Frameworks: Ethical frameworks provide structured approaches to analyzing dilemmas. Consider approaches like utilitarianism, deontology, virtue ethics, or ethical relativism. These frameworks guide your decision-making by considering factors like consequences, duties, virtues, and cultural context.

4. Consider Long-Term Consequences: Look beyond immediate outcomes and assess the long-term impact of your decisions. Consider how your choices might affect your reputation, relationships, and personal growth over time. Prioritize choices that contribute to sustainable, positive outcomes.

5. Engage in Open Dialogue: Discuss ethical challenges with those involved, inviting open and honest conversations. Sharing perspectives and concerns fosters understanding and may lead to collaborative solutions that consider the needs of all parties.

6. Consult Organizational Policies: If you're part of an organization, refer to its ethical guidelines and policies. These documents offer a framework for decision-making and can help you navigate dilemmas within the context of your workplace.

7. Seek a Third-Party Perspective: Engage an objective third party, such as an ethics committee or an external consultant, to provide an unbiased assessment of the situation. Their input can offer a fresh perspective and guide your decision-making process.

8. Consider the "Front Page" Test: Imagine your decision being publicized on the front page of a newspaper or social media. If you're uncomfortable with the idea of your choice being scrutinized by the public, it may indicate that the decision is ethically questionable.

9. Identify Alternatives: Explore alternative courses of action that align with your ethical principles. Sometimes, creativity can lead to solutions that satisfy ethical concerns while still achieving desired outcomes.

10. Take Responsibility and Accountability: Own your decisions and their consequences. Acknowledge any mistakes and take corrective actions if necessary. Demonstrating accountability reflects your commitment to ethical behavior.

11. Follow Your Gut Instinct: Pay attention to your intuition. If something doesn't feel right, it may indicate an ethical concern. Trusting your gut can guide you toward a decision that aligns with your values.

12. Consider Legal and Regulatory Aspects: Evaluate whether your decision complies with laws, regulations, and industry standards. Ethical decisions often align with legal requirements, but ethical behavior may go beyond what is strictly required by law.

13. Be Prepared to Stand Alone: In some cases, making an ethical decision may involve standing alone against opposition. Moral courage is vital when upholding principles in the face of resistance.

14. Continuous Learning and Improvement: Reflect on the outcomes of your decisions and learn from the experience. Over time, refine your approach to ethical challenges and apply the lessons learned to future dilemmas.

Ethical challenges are opportunities for growth, demonstrating your commitment to integrity and ethical behavior. By applying these strategies, you can navigate the moral maze with confidence, ensuring that your choices align with your values and contribute to a more responsible and ethical world.

Real-Life Case: Johnson & Johnson's Tylenol Crisis Management

Background: In the 1980s, Johnson & Johnson was a well-known and respected pharmaceutical company. However, the company faced a significant ethical and public relations crisis that tested its commitment to ethical decision-making.

The Situation: In 1982, seven people in the Chicago area died after consuming Extra-Strength Tylenol capsules that had been laced with cyanide. This incident shook public confidence in the safety of over-the-counter medications and posed a serious threat to Johnson & Johnson's reputation.

Ethical Decision-Making: Facing a potential catastrophe, Johnson & Johnson's leadership under CEO James Burke quickly took decisive and ethical actions. Instead of trying to downplay the issue or shift blame, the company prioritized the safety of its customers and the public.

Johnson & Johnson immediately launched a nationwide recall of 31 million bottles of Tylenol, costing the company an estimated $100 million. The decision was made to protect consumer safety and prevent further harm, even though it was a massive financial setback.

Transparency and Responsibility: Johnson & Johnson

communicated openly with the public, media, and law enforcement agencies. The company worked closely with the FBI, the FDA, and other authorities to assist in the investigation and find the person responsible for the tampering.

The company also introduced tamper-evident packaging and worked on new manufacturing processes to make the product safer. These actions demonstrated Johnson & Johnson's commitment to taking responsibility for the situation and ensuring that such an incident would not happen again.

The Impact: Johnson & Johnson's ethical decision-making and transparent crisis management efforts paid off. Despite the tragedy, the company's commitment to customer safety and responsible behavior was widely recognized and praised. The company rebuilt its reputation and regained consumer trust over time.

The Tylenol crisis became a case study in ethical decision-making and crisis management, showcasing how a company's commitment to doing what is right can lead to positive outcomes even in the face of a devastating situation.

Key Takeaways:

Prioritize Safety and Ethics: Johnson & Johnson's decision to prioritize consumer safety over financial considerations demonstrated ethical leadership.

Transparency and Responsibility: Open communication and taking responsibility are critical components of ethical decision-making during a crisis.

Long-Term Reputation: Upholding ethical values, even during challenging times, can contribute to rebuilding trust and reputation over time.

The Tylenol crisis is a real-life example of how ethical decision-making can carry the day and lead to positive outcomes even in the midst of a major crisis.

CHAPTER 6

Communication Ethics

*" To effectively communicate, we must realize
That we are all different in the way we perceive the world and use
this understanding as a guide to our communication with others"*

- Anthony Robbins

Building Trust and Integrity Through Effective Interaction

Communication is a fundamental aspect of human interaction, shaping relationships, conveying information, and influencing decisions. However, the power of communication comes with ethical responsibilities. Communication ethics encompasses the principles and standards that guide ethical behavior in all forms of communication, whether verbal, written, or digital. Upholding communication ethics is essential for fostering trust, promoting understanding, and maintaining integrity in personal, professional, and societal interactions.

Transparency and Truthfulness: Ethical communication hinges on transparency and truthfulness. Communicators have a responsibility to convey accurate information and avoid misinformation, distortion, or manipulation. Being forthright and honest builds trust and credibility in relationships.

Respect for Diversity and Inclusivity: Effective communication ethics embrace diverse perspectives and ensure inclusivity. Communicators must respect cultural differences, avoid stereotypes, and create an environment where all voices are heard and valued. By doing so, ethical communication contributes to a more inclusive and understanding society.

Privacy and Confidentiality: Respecting individuals' privacy and confidentiality is paramount in ethical communication. Communicators must seek permission before sharing personal information and refrain from disclosing confidential data without consent. This ensures that trust is maintained and personal boundaries are respected.

Avoiding Harm and Sensationalism: Ethical communicators prioritize the well-being of their audience. They refrain from disseminating content that may cause harm, sensationalize issues, or exploit vulnerabilities. Ethical communication aims to inform responsibly without compromising the emotional or psychological safety of recipients.

Accuracy and Fact-Checking: Ethical communication involves thorough fact-checking and verification of information before sharing it. Misinformation and fake news can have far-reaching consequences, eroding trust and creating confusion. Ethical communicators prioritize accuracy and reliability.

Balancing Freedom of Expression and Responsibility: While freedom of expression is a fundamental right, it's not absolute. Ethical communication balances this freedom with the responsibility to avoid hate speech, incitement to violence, and other harmful content that can undermine social harmony and well-being.

Cultural Sensitivity and Adaptation: Ethical communication is culturally sensitive. Communicators take into account cultural norms, values, and sensitivities when crafting messages. This ensures that communication is respectful and well-received across diverse audiences.

Open Dialogue and Listening: Ethical communication involves active listening and open dialogue. Communicators should engage in meaningful conversations, valuing diverse opinions and perspectives. This approach fosters understanding, empathy, and collaboration.

Digital Responsibility and Online Etiquette: In the digital age, ethical communication extends to online interactions. Ethical communicators practice digital responsibility, using social media and online platforms to share information responsibly, avoid cyberbullying, and contribute positively to online communities.

Empathy and Compassion: Ethical communication is rooted in empathy and compassion. Communicators strive to understand others' viewpoints, feelings, and experiences. By showing empathy, ethical communicators create connections and foster a sense of shared understanding.

Promoting Social Responsibility: Ethical communication has the power to promote social responsibility and positive change. Communicators can use their platform to raise awareness about social issues, advocate for justice, and inspire action that benefits society.

Building Lasting Relationships: Ethical communication is a cornerstone of building lasting relationships based on trust, mutual respect, and authenticity. Whether in personal, professional, or societal contexts, ethical communication ensures that interactions are guided by principles that enhance understanding, collaboration, and ethical behavior.

In a world where communication has the potential to shape perceptions and influence decisions, ethical communication becomes a powerful tool for fostering integrity, building trust, and contributing to a more just and ethical society. By adhering to communication ethics, individuals contribute to a communication landscape that reflects the values of honesty, respect, and responsible engagement.

Honest Communication: A Catalyst for Building Credibility

Credibility, the cornerstone of trust and influence, is nurtured through honest communication. In a world where information flows freely and skepticism abounds, cultivating credibility is essential for individuals, leaders, and organizations. Honest communication not only establishes authenticity but also strengthens relationships, fosters transparency, and paves the way for success.

Authenticity as a Foundation

Honest communication begins with authenticity. It involves aligning your words with your true thoughts, beliefs, and intentions. Authentic communication reflects your genuine self, resonating with others who value sincerity and transparency.

Imagine a leader who openly shares their challenges, setbacks, and lessons learned. Their authenticity invites trust from team members who appreciate their honesty and willingness to be vulnerable.

Transparency Fosters Trust

Honest communication goes hand in hand with transparency. Transparency means sharing information openly, whether it's good news or bad. When people perceive transparency, they feel respected and included, leading to the cultivation of trust.

Consider a company that openly communicates its financial status, both positive and negative. This transparency engenders trust among employees, investors, and customers, as they recognize the organization's commitment to honesty.

Consistency and Reliability

Consistency is key in building credibility. Consistently delivering accurate, truthful information establishes a track record of reliability. People trust those who consistently uphold their word and demonstrate integrity.

Imagine a colleague who consistently provides accurate updates on project progress. Their reliable communication style earns them the reputation of someone whose word can be trusted.

Admitting Mistakes and Learning

Honest communication includes admitting mistakes. Acknowledging errors demonstrates humility and a willingness to take responsibility. This openness to learning and growth enhances credibility.

Consider a professional who publicly acknowledges a mistake made in a presentation. Their honesty in admitting the error, along with their commitment to rectify it, enhances their credibility among peers and superiors.

Engaging Active Listening

Honest communication is a two-way street that involves active listening. When you genuinely listen to others' perspectives, concerns, and feedback, you signal respect and interest in understanding their viewpoints.

Imagine a manager who actively listens to employee feedback during team meetings. By valuing others' input and incorporating their ideas, this manager enhances their credibility as someone who values collaboration.

Confronting Difficult Conversations

Honest communication isn't always easy. It involves addressing difficult conversations with candor, while maintaining respect and empathy. Facing challenges head-on demonstrates courage and a commitment to open dialogue.

Consider a leader addressing a team about an impending restructuring. By openly discussing the situation, sharing reasons behind the decision, and acknowledging the potential impact, they exhibit honest communication that respects employees' need for information.

Building Lasting Relationships

Honest communication is the bedrock of lasting relationships. Whether in personal or professional contexts, individuals who communicate honestly build connections based on trust, respect, and mutual understanding.

Imagine a salesperson who openly discusses the pros and cons of a product, providing accurate information even when it might lead to a lost sale. This approach builds a reputation for honesty and fosters long-term customer loyalty.

In a world where credibility can make or break relationships and opportunities, honest communication emerges as a powerful catalyst. By embracing authenticity, transparency, consistency, humility, and active listening, individuals can shape a communication style that not only establishes credibility but also resonates with integrity and respect.

Ethical Persuasion: Influencing with Integrity

Persuasion is an art form that involves effectively communicating your ideas, convincing others to see your point of view, and inspiring them to take action. However, the ethical implications of persuasion are paramount, as influencing others should be guided by integrity, respect, and a commitment to shared values. Ethical persuasion is about using communication techniques that uphold honesty, transparency, and the well-being of all parties involved.

Shared Values and Common Ground

Ethical persuasion begins by identifying shared values and establishing common ground. When your message aligns with the values and interests of your audience, you build a foundation of trust and understanding.

Imagine a community organizer advocating for environmental conservation. By appealing to the shared value of preserving nature for future generations, they ethically persuade individuals to support their cause.

Honesty and Transparency

Ethical persuasion requires honesty and transparency. Present your ideas and information accurately, without exaggeration or manipulation. Integrity in your communication builds credibility and fosters trust.

Consider a marketing professional who promotes a product's benefits honestly while also mentioning its limitations. By providing a balanced perspective, they build trust with consumers and encourage informed decision-making.

Empathy and Understanding

Ethical persuasion involves understanding your audience's needs, concerns, and perspectives. Empathizing with their emotions and viewpoints enables you to tailor your message in a way that resonates with them.

Imagine a healthcare advocate discussing the importance of a healthy lifestyle. By acknowledging the challenges individuals face and empathizing with their struggles, they ethically persuade people to consider positive lifestyle changes.

Respect for Autonomy

Ethical persuasion respects individuals' autonomy and freedom of choice. While you may encourage certain actions, it's important to acknowledge that people have the right to make their own decisions.

Consider a financial advisor helping clients plan for retirement. Ethical persuasion involves presenting options and recommendations while also respecting clients' preferences and priorities.

Appealing to Reason and Emotion

Ethical persuasion balances logical reasoning with emotional appeal. Presenting rational arguments while also addressing emotional needs creates a well-rounded approach that considers both intellect and feelings.

Imagine a social worker advocating for funding to improve local schools. They present data on academic outcomes while also sharing personal stories of students who have benefited from better education. This approach engages both reason and empathy.

Providing Evidence and Credibility

Ethical persuasion relies on providing evidence and showcasing your credibility. Back your arguments with reliable sources, facts, and expertise to enhance the persuasiveness of your message.

Consider a scientist communicating the importance of climate change mitigation. By sharing peer-reviewed research and their own expertise, they ethically persuade others to take action to protect the environment.

Encouraging Informed Decision-Making

Ethical persuasion empowers individuals to make informed decisions. Present information comprehensively and allow your audience to critically evaluate the options presented.

Imagine a political candidate outlining their policy proposals.

Ethical persuasion involves providing detailed explanations and engaging in open debates, allowing voters to make informed choices based on a thorough understanding of the issues.

Ethical persuasion is a powerful tool that enables you to communicate effectively while upholding integrity. By focusing on shared values, honesty, empathy, and respect for autonomy, you can influence others ethically, fostering understanding, collaboration, and positive change.

Real-Life Case: The Volkswagen Emissions Scandal

Background: Volkswagen (VW) is a renowned German automobile manufacturer known for its innovation and engineering excellence. However, the company faced a significant communication ethics crisis that had far-reaching consequences.

The Situation: In 2015, it was revealed that Volkswagen had intentionally programmed its diesel vehicles' software to manipulate emissions tests. The software would detect when the car was undergoing an emissions test and temporarily reduce emissions to meet regulatory standards. Once the test was over, the software would revert to higher emission levels during normal driving, leading to significantly higher pollution levels.

Communication Ethics Lapses: The initial response from Volkswagen was marked by a lack of transparency and honesty. The company denied any wrongdoing and downplayed the significance of the emissions discrepancies. This response created confusion and eroded public trust as more evidence emerged.

Furthermore, Volkswagen's communication with regulators and customers lacked clarity and honesty, exacerbating the crisis. The company's lack of immediate accountability and transparency led to legal investigations, financial penalties, and a severe tarnishing of its reputation.

Recovery and Redemption: As the magnitude of the scandal became clear, Volkswagen faced a crossroads. The company recognized the need for a fundamental shift in communication ethics to regain trust and credibility.

Volkswagen's new leadership acknowledged the wrongdoing and implemented changes to address the ethical issues. The company cooperated with regulatory authorities, recalled millions of affected vehicles, and offered compensation to affected customers.

Volkswagen also launched a comprehensive communication campaign acknowledging the breach of trust and outlining its commitment to ethical behavior moving forward. This included transparency about corrective measures, changes in leadership, and plans for producing environmentally friendly vehicles.

The Impact: Volkswagen's initial communication ethics lapses had severe consequences, including legal penalties, fines, and damage to its reputation. However, the company's subsequent commitment to transparency, accountability, and ethical communication helped it begin the process of recovery.

The scandal served as a cautionary tale about the importance of ethical communication, especially during crises. It highlighted how a lack of honesty and transparency can exacerbate the impact of a crisis and erode public trust.

Key Takeaways:

Transparency Is Key: The Volkswagen case emphasizes the importance of transparency and honesty in communication, particularly during crises.

Ethical Recovery: Committing to ethical behavior and transparent communication can contribute to rebuilding trust and credibility over time.

<u>Consequences of Lapses:</u> Failure to uphold communication ethics can result in legal, financial, and reputational consequences.

The Volkswagen emissions scandal serves as a real-life case study highlighting the critical role of communication ethics in maintaining trust, mitigating damage, and setting a path toward recovery after a major ethical breach.

CHAPTER 7

Ethical Innovation and Creativity

*"The reconnection of society, economy and ethics
is a project we cannot postpone"*

- Michael D. Higgins

Navigating New Frontiers Responsibly

Innovation and creativity drive progress and propel societies forward, offering solutions to challenges and enriching lives. However, the pursuit of innovation must be guided by ethical considerations to ensure that new ideas, technologies, and creations bring about positive outcomes without causing harm. Ethical innovation and creativity involve pushing boundaries while maintaining a strong sense of responsibility, accountability, and respect for the well-being of individuals and the planet.

Anticipating Impact

Ethical innovation begins by anticipating the potential impact of new ideas and creations. Before introducing a novel product, technology, or concept, it's crucial to assess how it might affect individuals, communities, the environment, and society at large.

Imagine a tech company developing an app that collects personal data for targeted advertising. Ethical innovation requires evaluating how this data collection might compromise user privacy and exploring ways to mitigate potential risks.

Solving Real-World Problems

Ethical innovation is driven by a commitment to solving real-world problems. Innovators seek to address societal challenges, improve quality of life, and create positive change rather than simply chasing profit or recognition.

Consider a team of engineers designing affordable and energy-efficient housing solutions for underserved communities. Their ethical innovation aims to address a pressing social issue while considering the local environment and cultural context.

Sustainability and Long-Term Vision

Ethical innovation is inherently sustainable, considering the long-term consequences of new ideas and technologies. Innovators focus on creating solutions that endure over time, minimizing negative impacts on resources and ecosystems.

Imagine a company developing a new packaging material that is biodegradable and reduces waste. Ethical innovation aligns with a long-term vision of sustainability, reducing the ecological footprint of the product.

Inclusion and Diversity

Ethical innovation embraces inclusion and diversity. Innovators recognize that a wide range of perspectives leads to more comprehensive problem-solving and ensures that the benefits of innovation are accessible to all segments of society.

Consider a team working on medical device design. Ethical innovation involves including diverse voices, including those of patients and healthcare professionals, to ensure that the final product meets the needs of a wide range of users.

Ethical Considerations in AI and Automation

In the realm of artificial intelligence and automation, ethical innovation is particularly vital. Innovators must ensure that AI systems are unbiased, transparent, and accountable, and that they respect privacy and human autonomy.

Imagine a company developing an AI-powered recruitment tool. Ethical innovation involves addressing biases in the algorithm that might perpetuate discrimination and ensuring that the technology adheres to fair and ethical hiring practices.

Collaboration and Stakeholder Engagement

Ethical innovation thrives on collaboration and engagement with stakeholders. Innovators actively involve those who will be impacted by their creations, seeking input, feedback, and insights to ensure that ethical considerations are prioritized.

Consider a company launching a new energy-efficient transportation solution. Ethical innovation involves consulting local communities, policymakers, and environmental experts to ensure that the solution aligns with local needs and sustainable practices.

Ethics in Creative Expression

In creative fields, ethical considerations guide the messages and content that artists and creators produce. Ethical creativity involves questioning how their work may influence perceptions, values, and cultural dynamics.

Imagine a filmmaker depicting sensitive social issues in their work. Ethical creativity entails representing these issues authentically, responsibly, and with consideration for potential impact on viewers' perspectives.

Continuous Ethical Assessment

Ethical innovation is an ongoing process that involves continuous assessment and adaptation. As technologies evolve and societal contexts change, innovators must revisit their creations to ensure they remain aligned with ethical principles.

Consider a company that produces electronic devices. Ethical innovation necessitates regularly evaluating the environmental impact of their products, exploring ways to reduce waste and promote recycling.

Ethical innovation and creativity hold the potential to transform the world for the better. By embracing ethical considerations as an integral part of the innovation process, individuals and organizations can pave the way for progress that is responsible, sustainable, and inclusive.

Ethics in Innovation: Pioneering Responsibly and Sustainably

Innovation, the driving force behind progress, has the potential to revolutionize industries, enhance lives, and shape the future. However, the path of innovation is not without its ethical challenges. As pioneers forge ahead with groundbreaking ideas and technologies, the importance of ethics in innovation becomes paramount. Ethics in innovation involves navigating uncharted territories with a strong moral compass, ensuring that new frontiers are explored responsibly, sustainably, and with the well-being of individuals and the environment in mind.

Human-Centric Innovation

Ethics in innovation begins by putting humans at the center of the equation. Innovators must prioritize the impact of their creations on individuals' lives, respecting their rights, autonomy, and well-being. Human-centric innovation seeks to enhance the human experience while minimizing harm.

Imagine a biotech company developing a new medical treatment. Ethical innovation ensures that rigorous testing is conducted to ensure the treatment's safety and efficacy before it is introduced to patients.

Environmental Responsibility

Innovation should consider its ecological footprint. Ethical innovators recognize the interconnectedness of the planet and strive to minimize negative environmental impacts. They seek sustainable solutions that mitigate harm to ecosystems and contribute to a healthier planet.

Consider a company developing renewable energy technologies. Ethical innovation involves considering the entire life cycle of these technologies, from production to disposal, to ensure they align with sustainability goals.

Anticipating Unintended Consequences

Ethics in innovation involves foreseeing and addressing unintended consequences. Innovators must conduct thorough risk assessments to identify potential negative impacts on individuals, society, and the environment. Proactively addressing these issues prevents harm and supports responsible progress.

Imagine a tech company introducing a new communication platform. Ethical innovation involves anticipating potential misuse that could lead to cyberbullying and implementing safeguards to prevent harm.

Respect for Privacy and Data Security

Innovative technologies often collect and process personal data. Ethics in innovation demands respect for privacy and data security. Innovators must prioritize robust data protection measures and transparent data usage practices to maintain individuals' trust.

Consider a company developing smart home devices. Ethical innovation involves implementing strong encryption and clear data usage policies to safeguard users' personal information.

Equity and Accessibility

Ethical innovation ensures that benefits are accessible to all, regardless of socioeconomic status, geography, or background. Innovators must consider how their creations might inadvertently exacerbate inequalities and work to bridge these gaps.

Imagine a team creating educational technology for remote learning. Ethical innovation involves providing access to resources for underserved communities, ensuring that all students have equal opportunities to learn.

Transparency and Informed Consent

Innovators should be transparent about their intentions and the potential risks of their innovations. Ethical innovation involves obtaining informed consent from stakeholders who might be affected, allowing them to make informed decisions.

Consider a company developing facial recognition technology. Ethical innovation requires transparently communicating its potential applications and obtaining explicit consent before implementing the technology in public spaces.

Social Impact and Responsibility

Ethical innovation involves considering broader societal implications. Innovators must ask themselves how their creations might shape cultural dynamics, norms, and values, and whether these changes are aligned with ethical principles.

Imagine a social media platform introducing a new algorithm. Ethical innovation involves evaluating how the algorithm might influence users' behavior and emotions, ensuring that it promotes positive interactions.

Collaboration and Stakeholder Engagement

Ethical innovation thrives on collaboration and engagement

with stakeholders. Innovators must involve those who will be impacted by their creations, seeking diverse perspectives and feedback to ensure that ethical considerations are integrated into the innovation process.

Consider a company developing autonomous vehicles. Ethical innovation involves engaging with regulators, transportation experts, and the public to collectively address ethical dilemmas related to safety and decision-making algorithms.

Ongoing Ethical Evaluation

Ethics in innovation is not a one-time consideration; it requires continuous evaluation. As technologies evolve and societal contexts change, ethical innovators must revisit their creations, adapt to new challenges, and uphold their commitment to responsible progress.

Consider a tech startup developing artificial intelligence applications. Ethical innovation involves regularly assessing the ethical implications of their algorithms, training data, and potential biases to ensure fairness and inclusivity.

Innovation has the potential to reshape the world, but it must be guided by a strong ethical foundation. By embracing ethics in innovation, pioneers can navigate uncharted territories responsibly, safeguarding the well-being of individuals, communities, and the environment, while shaping a future that is both advanced and ethically sound.

Fostering Ethical Creativity in a Competitive World

In a rapidly evolving and competitive world, creativity is a powerful asset that drives innovation and sets individuals and organizations apart. However, the pursuit of creativity must be underpinned by strong ethical values to ensure that original ideas and solutions contribute positively to society. Fostering ethical creativity involves cultivating a mindset that encourages both imaginative thinking and responsible behavior, even in the face of challenges and competition.

Aligning Creativity with Values

Ethical creativity begins with aligning creative pursuits with personal and organizational values. Creatives must consider how their ideas and innovations reflect their principles and contribute to the greater good.

Imagine an advertising agency tasked with promoting a product. Ethical creativity involves crafting campaigns that are both imaginative and truthful, avoiding exaggerations or misleading information.

Respecting Boundaries and Integrity

Ethical creativity respects boundaries and upholds integrity. Creatives must innovate within ethical constraints, avoiding ideas that could compromise the rights, privacy, or well-being of individuals.

Consider a content creator developing an online video. Ethical creativity involves avoiding content that perpetuates harmful stereotypes or violates others' rights, even if it might attract attention.

Embracing Inclusivity and Diversity

Ethical creativity values inclusivity and diversity. Creatives should actively seek input and perspectives from a wide range of backgrounds, ensuring that their ideas reflect the richness of human experiences.

Imagine a design team developing a new app. Ethical creativity involves considering the needs and preferences of diverse users to create an inclusive and user-friendly interface.

Balancing Innovation and Responsibility

Ethical creativity involves striking a balance between innovation and responsibility. Creatives must push boundaries while also considering potential consequences and unintended outcomes.

Consider a tech startup developing new artificial intelligence technology. Ethical creativity involves exploring novel applications while ensuring that the technology adheres to ethical standards and does not perpetuate biases.

Questioning and Critical Thinking

Ethical creativity thrives on questioning and critical thinking. Creatives should challenge assumptions, evaluate potential risks, and consider the broader impact of their ideas.

Imagine a writer crafting a fictional story with controversial themes. Ethical creativity involves examining how the narrative might influence readers' perceptions and attitudes and considering ways to address sensitive issues responsibly.

Ethics as a Source of Inspiration

Ethical creativity draws inspiration from ethical dilemmas and challenges. Creatives can find innovative solutions that tackle real-world problems while upholding their values.

Consider a fashion designer creating sustainable clothing. Ethical creativity involves designing stylish and eco-friendly garments that address both fashion trends and environmental concerns.

Collaboration and Shared Goals

Ethical creativity thrives in collaborative environments where diverse perspectives converge. Creatives should work together toward shared goals that prioritize ethical considerations.

Imagine a team of scientists developing medical breakthroughs. Ethical creativity involves collaborating to ensure that research aligns with ethical principles and has a positive impact on patients' lives.

Educating and Nurturing Ethical Creatives

Fostering ethical creativity requires education and nurturing from early stages. Educational institutions, mentors, and organizations should emphasize the importance of ethics alongside creative skills.

Imagine an art school incorporating ethical discussions into its curriculum. Ethical creativity involves encouraging students to explore thought-provoking themes while considering the ethical implications of their art.

Championing Ethical Role Models

Ethical creativity gains strength from the examples set by role models who blend creativity and ethics seamlessly. Individuals who prioritize ethical considerations in their creative pursuits inspire others to do the same.

Imagine a renowned filmmaker known for producing thought-provoking films that address ethical dilemmas. Their ethical creativity sets an example for aspiring filmmakers to use their craft as a means of ethical exploration and expression.

Sustainability as a Guiding Principle

Ethical creativity often aligns with sustainability. Creatives should consider the environmental and social impact of their work, striving for solutions that endure and contribute positively to society.

Consider a startup developing innovative packaging materials. Ethical creativity involves designing materials that are both functional and environmentally friendly, reducing waste and promoting sustainability.

In a competitive world, ethical creativity stands as a

beacon of innovation that upholds integrity, values, and societal well-being. By nurturing a culture that values both imaginative thinking and ethical responsibility, individuals and organizations can contribute to a future where creativity and ethics go hand in hand, shaping progress that is not only cutting-edge but also responsible and sustainable.

Real-Life Case: Patagonia's Worn Wear Program

Background: Patagonia is a well-known outdoor clothing and gear company with a strong commitment to environmental sustainability and ethical practices. The company's approach to ethical innovation and creativity is exemplified by its "Worn Wear" program.

The Situation: In the fast-paced fashion industry, many companies focus on encouraging consumers to buy new products, contributing to the issue of textile waste and environmental degradation. Patagonia recognized the environmental impact of over-consumption and sought to challenge the norm through ethical innovation.

Ethical Innovation: Patagonia launched the Worn Wear program in 2013 as a way to promote the repair, reuse, and recycling of its products. The program encourages customers to bring back their old and worn Patagonia clothing and gear for repair or exchange. This initiative aligns with the company's commitment to reducing waste, promoting sustainability, and extending the lifespan of its products.

Instead of treating worn-out items as disposable, Patagonia sees them as an opportunity for creative problem-solving. The company's repair technicians work to fix damaged items, and those that can't be repaired are recycled to create new products, such as recycled polyester fibers.

Creative Consumer Engagement: Patagonia's Worn Wear

program goes beyond the traditional approach to business. It encourages consumers to value their products for their longevity and quality, rather than promoting constant consumption. The company even celebrates the stories behind the well-worn items, highlighting the adventures and memories associated with them.

Patagonia also hosts Worn Wear events and pop-up repair shops, where customers can have their products repaired on the spot and learn more about sustainability. This engages consumers in a creative and educational way while promoting responsible consumption.

The Impact: The Worn Wear program has had a significant impact on Patagonia's brand image and the industry as a whole. The company's commitment to ethical innovation and sustainability has resonated with consumers who appreciate its dedication to minimizing environmental impact.

The program has also sparked conversations about the fashion industry's responsibility to address waste and promote ethical practices. Patagonia's approach to ethical innovation showcases how creativity and a commitment to sustainability can lead to positive change and inspire others in the industry to follow suit.

Key Takeaways:

Innovating Ethical Practices: Patagonia's Worn Wear program demonstrates how ethical innovation can drive sustainability and challenge industry norms.

Creative Consumer Engagement: Engaging consumers in creative ways can promote responsible consumption and create a sense of shared values.

Positive Industry Influence: Ethical innovation can have a ripple effect, inspiring others in the industry to adopt more sustainable practices.

Patagonia's Worn Wear program is a real-life case study that showcases how ethical innovation and creativity can reshape an industry's approach to consumption and sustainability, fostering a deeper connection between a company, its products, and its consumers.

CHAPTER 8

Ethical Personal Growth

"Knowing others is intelligence. Knowing yourself is true wisdom. Mastering others is strength. Mastering yourself is true power"

- Lao Tzu

Nurturing Character and Integrity

Personal growth is a journey of self-discovery, self-improvement, and transformation. While pursuing growth, it's essential to align this journey with ethical principles that guide your actions and decisions. Ethical personal growth involves not only enhancing your skills and capabilities but also cultivating virtues, values, and a sense of integrity that contribute to your well-being and the betterment of society.

Self-Reflection and Values Clarification

Ethical personal growth begins with self-reflection and values clarification. Take time to understand your core values and beliefs, and consider how they align with your goals and aspirations. This self-awareness forms the foundation for your growth journey.

Imagine an individual seeking personal growth who reflects

on their values and realizes that compassion and empathy are central to who they are. They then focus their growth efforts on enhancing these qualities to foster meaningful connections with others.

Continuous Learning and Development

Ethical personal growth involves continuous learning and development. As you acquire new skills and knowledge, ensure that your growth extends beyond the realm of expertise and also includes personal character and ethical awareness.

Consider a professional pursuing career growth by taking leadership courses. Ethical personal growth entails not only learning leadership techniques but also developing qualities like honesty, transparency, and empathy to lead with integrity.

Balancing Ambition and Ethics

Ethical personal growth strikes a balance between ambition and ethics. While aiming for success and achievement, remain mindful of the ethical implications of your choices and actions. Consider how your growth journey impacts others and the broader community.

Imagine an entrepreneur striving for business success. Ethical personal growth involves pursuing innovation and profitability while also considering the social and environmental consequences of their business practices.

Cultivating Virtues and Integrity

Ethical personal growth involves cultivating virtues that shape your character. Virtues like honesty, compassion, humility, and resilience contribute to a strong moral foundation that guides your decisions and interactions.

Consider an individual working on personal growth who actively cultivates the virtue of integrity. They consistently uphold their values, align their actions with their words, and make decisions that reflect their ethical principles.

Embracing Empathy and Social Responsibility

Ethical personal growth extends beyond self-interest to embrace empathy and social responsibility. Consider how your personal growth journey can positively impact others and contribute to the well-being of your community.

Imagine a student focusing on personal growth who volunteers at a local shelter. Ethical personal growth involves not only enhancing their own skills but also using their growth journey to support others and address societal needs.

Mindful Decision-Making

Ethical personal growth involves mindful decision-making. As you navigate choices and opportunities, consider the ethical implications and the potential consequences for yourself and others. Make decisions that align with your values and principles.

Consider an individual presented with a career opportunity in a cigarette company, and this conflicts with his ethical beliefs of no harm to himself and others. Ethical personal growth involves the courage to decline the opportunity, prioritizing integrity over personal gain.

Accountability and Reflection

Ethical personal growth entails accountability and reflection. Regularly assess your growth journey to ensure that you're staying true to your values and ethical principles. Acknowledge your mistakes and learn from them, using setbacks as opportunities for growth.

Imagine someone committed to ethical personal growth who, after a setback, takes time to reflect on their actions and learns from their mistakes. This introspection fuels their determination to continue growing ethically.

Inspiring Others Through Ethical Growth

Ethical personal growth can inspire others to embark on their own growth journeys. When people witness your commitment to ethical values and personal development, they may be encouraged to align their growth with ethics as well.

Imagine a leader in a workplace who demonstrates ethical personal growth by fostering a culture of respect, collaboration, and transparency. Their example encourages colleagues to pursue growth that elevates both their skills and ethical consciousness.

Ethical personal growth is a profound endeavor that integrates self-improvement with ethical principles. By aligning your growth journey with virtues, values, and integrity, you contribute to your own well-being while also fostering a positive impact on the world around you.

Self-Development: Nurturing Character and Virtue

Self-development is a journey of intentional growth that encompasses not only the enhancement of skills and knowledge but also the cultivation of character and virtue. It involves striving for personal excellence while embracing qualities that reflect your true self and contribute positively to your interactions with others and the world. Nurturing character and virtue within the realm of self-development elevates your journey to one of holistic growth and ethical living.

Defining Character and Virtue

Character refers to the collection of traits and qualities that define who you are at your core. Virtue, on the other hand, encompasses moral excellence and ethical qualities that guide your behavior and interactions. Self-development offers an opportunity to nurture these aspects of yourself intentionally.

Imagine an individual working on self-development who values compassion, honesty, and resilience. They actively cultivate these virtues as they pursue personal growth.

Values-Driven Self-Development

Self-development gains depth and purpose when it's driven by your values. Identifying your core values serves as a compass for your growth journey, ensuring that your actions and choices align with your ethical principles.

Consider someone focused on self-development who values integrity and authenticity. Their growth journey involves consistently aligning their actions with these values, even when faced with challenges.

Cultivating Virtues

Virtues are qualities that shape your character and guide your behavior. Self-development involves intentionally cultivating virtues that enhance your ethical compass and contribute to your personal growth.

Imagine an individual committed to self-development who actively works on cultivating patience, empathy, and gratitude. These virtues not only enrich their personal well-being but also positively impact their relationships with others.

Balancing Skill Enhancement and Virtuous Living

Self-development often includes skill enhancement and knowledge acquisition. Balancing these aspects with the cultivation of virtues ensures that your growth journey enriches both your abilities and your character.

Consider a professional pursuing self-development in their career. In addition to improving their technical skills, they also prioritize virtues like teamwork, humility, and ethical decision-making.

Reflective Practice

Self-development involves reflective practice, where you regularly assess your growth journey. Reflecting on your actions, choices, and progress allows you to make adjustments, acknowledge areas for improvement, and reinforce your commitment to virtues.

Imagine an individual engaged in self-development who sets aside time for introspection and journaling. Through this reflective practice, they gain insights into their journey and make conscious decisions to enhance their character.

Accountability and Responsibility

Self-development is characterized by accountability and responsibility. You hold yourself responsible for your growth, ensuring that you're not only enhancing your skills but also living in accordance with your chosen virtues.

Consider someone on a journey of self-development who takes ownership of their actions and decisions. They embrace accountability for their mistakes and actively work on rectifying them, aligning with their commitment to virtues.

Inspiring Others through Exemplary Growth

Self-development that nurtures character and virtue has the power to inspire others. When people witness your commitment to ethical principles and virtuous living, they may be encouraged to embark on their own growth journeys with similar intentions.

Imagine an individual who demonstrates self-development through virtues like compassion and generosity. Their actions inspire those around them to reflect on their own growth journeys and consider how they can contribute positively to others.

Contributing to a Better World

Self-development that focuses on character and virtue contributes to a better world. When individuals prioritize ethical qualities in their growth journeys, they collectively contribute to a more compassionate, just, and empathetic society.

Consider a group of individuals engaged in self-development who collectively foster a culture of kindness, respect, and ethical behavior. Their commitment to nurturing character and virtue creates a ripple effect that positively impacts their communities.

Self-development is a transformative journey that encompasses more than skill acquisition; it's an opportunity to nurture character, embrace virtues, and live ethically. By aligning your growth with values and virtues, you create a path to personal excellence that not only benefits you but also radiates positive influence to those around you.

Ethical Self-Care: Balancing Ambition with Well-being

In a world that often glorifies busyness and achievement, the concept of self-care has emerged as a vital practice for maintaining overall well-being. However, ethical self-care takes this idea a step further by emphasizing the importance of balancing personal ambition and success with a commitment to ethical values, integrity, and the well-being of oneself and others. Ethical self-care recognizes that achieving goals and pursuing excellence should be harmonized with ethical considerations and the cultivation of a compassionate, responsible, and balanced lifestyle. Throwing away your health for instance in pursuit of success will definitely undermine the value of the success gained.

Defining Ethical Self-Care

Ethical self-care involves intentionally practicing self-care in a way that aligns with ethical principles and values. It encompasses actions and choices that not only prioritize your own well-being but also consider the well-being of others, your community, and the environment.

Imagine an individual practicing ethical self-care who not only focuses on their physical health but also engages in acts of kindness that benefit their community, demonstrating a commitment to ethical living.

Balancing Ambition and Well-being

Ethical self-care addresses the balance between ambition and well-being. While pursuing personal and professional goals is essential, it should not come at the expense of physical, emotional, or ethical well-being.

Consider a professional striving for career advancement who also makes time for regular exercise, relaxation, and ethical decision-making. Ethical self-care ensures that ambition is balanced with self-compassion and ethical considerations.

Prioritizing Holistic Well-being

Ethical self-care encompasses holistic well-being, which includes physical, emotional, social, and ethical dimensions. Nurturing these aspects of well-being promotes a balanced and fulfilling life.

Imagine an individual practicing ethical self-care who dedicates time to exercise, maintains healthy relationships, engages in self-reflection, and consistently acts in alignment with their values.

Mindful Time Management

Ethical self-care involves mindful time management. While pursuing ambitions and goals, allocate time for self-care practices that support your well-being and ethical values.

Consider someone balancing work responsibilities with ethical self-care practices like volunteering or spending quality time with loved ones, ensuring that their time is spent in ways that nurture both their goals and well-being.

Setting Ethical Boundaries

Ethical self-care requires setting ethical boundaries. Clearly define limits that prevent overexertion, unethical behavior, or compromising values in the pursuit of success.

Imagine a professional who sets an ethical boundary by refusing to engage in deceptive marketing practices, even if it could potentially lead to short-term gains. This decision reflects their commitment to ethical self-care.

Respecting Ethical Priorities

Ethical self-care involves respecting ethical priorities over external pressures. It means making choices that align with your values, even when faced with societal expectations or competing demands.

Consider an individual who turns down an opportunity that conflicts with their ethical values, prioritizing their integrity and well-being over external recognition or rewards.

Embracing Rest and Reflection

Ethical self-care recognizes the value of rest and reflection. Taking time to rest, recharge, and engage in self-reflection contributes to mental and emotional well-being and supports ethical decision-making.

Imagine a busy professional who practices ethical self-care by incorporating regular periods of rest and relaxation into their routine, allowing themselves time to rejuvenate and reflect on their ethical journey.

Fostering Compassion and Empathy

Ethical self-care involves fostering compassion and empathy, not only toward oneself but also toward others. Practicing kindness and understanding supports both personal well-being and ethical interconnectedness.

Consider someone who practices ethical self-care by participating in community service and supporting charitable causes, extending their care beyond themselves and contributing to the well-being of others.

Ethical self-care is a harmonious approach to well-being that recognizes the interconnectedness of personal ambition, ethical principles, and holistic wellness. By prioritizing ethical considerations and nurturing your physical, emotional, and social dimensions of well-being, you create a life that is not only successful but also compassionate, meaningful, and ethically grounded.

Real-Life Case: Malala Yousafzai's Journey of Ethical Personal Growth

Background: Malala Yousafzai is a Pakistani education activist known for her advocacy of girls' education and her commitment to social justice. Her remarkable journey showcases the power of ethical personal growth in the face of adversity.

The Situation: In 2012, Malala was targeted by the Taliban for advocating girls' education in the Swat Valley of Pakistan. She was shot in the head and narrowly survived the assassination attempt. The incident brought international attention to her cause and turned her into a global symbol of courage and resilience.

Ethical Personal Growth: Malala's response to the attack demonstrated remarkable ethical personal growth. Instead of succumbing to fear or hatred, she emerged from the experience with even greater determination to fight for education and gender equality. She channeled her pain and adversity into a powerful force for positive change.

Malala's commitment to her values and her desire to make a difference led her to establish the Malala Fund, an organization dedicated to promoting girls' education worldwide. She continued to speak out against injustice and oppression, inspiring millions with her courage and eloquence.

Empathy and Advocacy: Malala's ethical personal growth was marked by her ability to empathize with others who faced similar challenges. Despite her own traumatic experience, she remained deeply connected to the struggles of those without a platform or voice. She consistently advocated for the rights of marginalized individuals, including refugees and young girls facing discrimination.

The Impact: Malala's journey of ethical personal growth has had a profound impact on the global stage. She became the youngest-ever recipient of the Nobel Peace Prize in 2014, further amplifying her advocacy and giving her message an even broader reach.

Her story continues to inspire people around the world to stand up for their beliefs, to overcome adversity, and to pursue ethical personal growth even in the face of unimaginable challenges.

Key Takeaways:

Turning Adversity into Purpose: Malala's story demonstrates how ethical personal growth can arise from adversity and be channeled into a powerful force for positive change.

Commitment to Values: Remaining committed to one's values and beliefs, even in the face of danger, can lead to remarkable personal growth and impact.

Empathy and Advocacy: Ethical personal growth can include a

heightened sense of empathy and a commitment to advocating for the rights and well-being of others.

Malala Yousafzai's journey of ethical personal growth serves as a real-life case study that exemplifies the transformative power of staying true to one's values, advocating for justice, and using personal experiences to drive meaningful change on a global scale.

CHAPTER 9

Ethical Success in Business

"Never deceive others, in business or in life. In 1995, I was deceived by four companies - four companies that are now closed. A company cannot go far by deceit."

- Jack Ma

Building Prosperity with Integrity

Business success is often measured in financial terms, but ethical success goes beyond profits to encompass integrity, responsibility, and the positive impact a business has on its stakeholders and the broader community. Ethical success involves pursuing excellence while upholding ethical values and principles, fostering a culture of transparency, fairness, and social responsibility. It's about creating prosperity in a way that aligns with ethical considerations, leaving a lasting positive legacy for all those affected by the business.

Balancing Profit and Ethics

Ethical success requires striking a balance between financial gains and ethical considerations. While profitability is important, ethical businesses prioritize responsible practices that contribute positively to society, the environment, and the well-being of employees and customers.

Imagine a company that manufactures eco-friendly products. Ethical success involves not only generating profits but also minimizing environmental impact, promoting sustainability, and providing consumers with ethically produced goods.

Ethical Leadership and Culture

Ethical success begins with ethical leadership. Leaders set the tone for the entire organization, fostering a culture of honesty, respect, and accountability. A business culture that values ethical behavior and decision-making becomes a foundation for long-term success.

Consider a CEO who leads by example, making transparent decisions, treating employees fairly, and upholding the highest ethical standards. Under this leadership, the company's culture becomes synonymous with integrity.

Stakeholder Engagement and Trust

Ethical success involves engaging with stakeholders openly and transparently. Building trust with customers, employees, investors, suppliers, and the community is crucial for sustained success.

Imagine a business that proactively communicates its sustainability efforts, engages in fair trade practices, and supports local communities. Ethical success is achieved when stakeholders trust the company's commitment to ethical practices.

Social Responsibility and Community Impact

Ethical success extends beyond profit margins to social responsibility. Businesses that contribute positively to their communities and address societal challenges earn ethical success through their impact on people's lives.

Consider a company that allocates resources for charitable initiatives, mentors local youth, and supports community development projects. Ethical success involves leveraging business resources to create positive social change.

Ethical Innovation and Problem Solving

Ethical success includes innovative problem-solving that respects ethical boundaries. Businesses can innovate while considering the potential consequences of their solutions on individuals, society, and the environment.

Imagine a tech company developing artificial intelligence solutions. Ethical success involves ensuring that AI technologies respect privacy, avoid biases, and align with ethical guidelines.

Transparency and Accountability

Ethical success hinges on transparency and accountability. Businesses that communicate openly about their practices, successes, and challenges are more likely to earn the trust of stakeholders and demonstrate their commitment to ethical behavior.

Consider a business that regularly publishes sustainability reports, detailing their environmental impact and social initiatives. Ethical success is achieved when stakeholders can easily access information about the company's ethical practices.

Ethical Supply Chain and Partnerships

Ethical success involves extending ethical considerations to supply chains and partnerships. Businesses should collaborate with suppliers, distributors, and partners who share their commitment to ethical practices.

Imagine a company sourcing materials from suppliers who adhere to fair labor practices and environmental standards. Ethical success is achieved by creating a supply chain that reflects the company's ethical values.

Long-Term Sustainability and Legacy

Ethical success is sustainable success. Businesses that prioritize ethical considerations in their operations and decision-making create a legacy of positive impact that endures beyond short-term financial gains.

Consider a family-owned business that passes down ethical values through generations, ensuring the company's continued commitment to ethical practices and making a lasting contribution to society.

Positive Impact on Society

Ethical success in business isn't solely measured by financial achievements. It's about the positive impact a business has on society, leaving a mark that extends beyond the balance sheet.

Imagine a business that provides fair wages, invests in employee development, and supports local initiatives. Ethical success is achieved when the business improves the lives of its employees and contributes to the well-being of the community.

Ethical success in business isn't just an aspiration; it's a responsibility. By combining prosperity with integrity, businesses can create a positive impact that resonates with stakeholders and society, fostering long-term success built on a foundation of ethical principles.

Business Ethics: Ethical Practices for Sustainable Profitability

Business ethics forms the cornerstone of responsible and sustainable profitability. In an interconnected world where consumers and stakeholders demand transparency, fairness, and ethical conduct, businesses that prioritize ethics not only thrive financially but also build lasting relationships and contribute positively to society. Ethical practices not only guide day-to-day operations but also shape a business's reputation, impact, and long-term success.

Integrity as the Foundation

Integrity is at the heart of business ethics. Ethical practices begin with a commitment to honesty, transparency, and the consistent alignment of actions with values. Businesses that prioritize integrity build trust with stakeholders, fostering a reputation that's essential for sustainable profitability.

Imagine a company that refuses to compromise on product quality to cut costs. By maintaining integrity and consistently delivering quality, the company earns customer loyalty and a solid reputation for ethical conduct.

Fair and Ethical Treatment

Business ethics encompasses fair treatment of all stakeholders. This includes employees, customers, suppliers, investors, and the broader community. Ethical businesses value diversity, ensure equal opportunities, and provide a safe and respectful environment for everyone involved.

Consider a company that promotes diversity in its workforce and enforces zero tolerance for discrimination. Ethical treatment fosters a positive workplace culture and attracts a diverse pool of talent.

Responsible Environmental Stewardship

Ethical business practices extend to environmental responsibility. Sustainable profitability involves minimizing negative impacts on the environment, conserving resources, and actively pursuing eco-friendly initiatives.

Imagine a business that invests in renewable energy sources, reduces waste, and implements sustainable packaging practices. Ethical environmental practices not only demonstrate corporate responsibility but also resonate with environmentally conscious consumers.

Transparent Corporate Governance

Ethical business practices are reflected in transparent corporate governance. Businesses with clear structures, ethical decision-making processes, and mechanisms to prevent corruption uphold accountability and ensure that decisions are made in the best interest of all stakeholders.

Consider a company that regularly discloses financial information, adheres to ethical codes of conduct, and maintains an independent board of directors. Transparent governance builds investor trust and promotes ethical practices.

Customer-Centric Approach

Ethical business practices emphasize a customer-centric approach. Businesses prioritize providing accurate information, delivering quality products and services, and addressing customer concerns promptly and honestly.

Imagine a business that offers a money-back guarantee for dissatisfied customers. This customer-centric approach not only builds trust but also enhances customer loyalty, ultimately contributing to sustainable profitability.

Ethical Marketing and Advertising

Ethical business practices extend to marketing and advertising efforts. Businesses should avoid deceptive practices, false claims, and manipulative techniques that mislead or exploit consumers.

Consider a company that markets its products honestly, using accurate information and avoiding exaggerations. Ethical marketing builds credibility and fosters a loyal customer base.

Social Responsibility Initiatives

Ethical businesses engage in social responsibility initiatives that contribute positively to society. They invest in charitable activities, support community development, and address pressing social issues.

Imagine a business that sponsors educational programs for underprivileged children in its community. Social responsibility not only benefits the community but also enhances the business's reputation and brand image.

Ethical Supply Chain Management

Ethical practices extend to supply chain management. Businesses should ensure that suppliers adhere to ethical labor practices, environmental standards, and human rights principles.

Consider a company that conducts regular audits of its suppliers to verify ethical compliance. Ethical supply chain management reflects a commitment to responsible business practices throughout the entire value chain.

Long-Term Impact and Legacy

Ethical business practices aren't just about short-term profitability; they shape a business's long-term impact and legacy. Businesses that prioritize ethics contribute to a positive and sustainable legacy that extends beyond financial gains.

Imagine a business that creates scholarship programs for local students, leaving a lasting impact on education in its community. Ethical practices create a legacy of positive change and long-term relevance.

Ethical practices and sustainable profitability are intertwined. By integrating ethics into every aspect of their operations, businesses can achieve profitability while also earning the trust, respect, and loyalty of stakeholders. Ethical business practices not only drive financial success but also ensure a positive impact on the world and leave a meaningful legacy for generations to come.

Building Ethical Brands: Trust and Loyalty as Accelerators

In a world characterized by increasing consumer awareness and a desire for responsible consumption, building ethical brands has become not only a moral imperative but also a strategic advantage. Ethical brands prioritize transparency, social responsibility, and environmental stewardship, earning the trust and loyalty of consumers. Trust and loyalty, when nurtured through ethical practices, become powerful accelerators that drive brand success, sustainable growth, and a positive impact on society.

The Power of Trust

Trust is the cornerstone of ethical branding. Consumers are more likely to support brands they trust to deliver on promises, act transparently, and prioritize ethical considerations. Trust builds a strong foundation for meaningful connections between brands and consumers.

Imagine a clothing brand that discloses its supply chain, from raw materials to manufacturing, ensuring fair labor practices. This commitment to transparency fosters trust and resonates with consumers who prioritize ethical consumption.

Transparency and Authenticity

Ethical brands thrive on transparency and authenticity. Brands that openly share information about their practices, values, and impact create a sense of authenticity that resonates with consumers seeking genuine connections.

Consider a food company that provides detailed information about the sourcing of its ingredients and the steps taken to minimize environmental impact. Transparent communication builds authenticity and instills confidence in consumers.

Social Responsibility and Community Engagement

Ethical brands engage in social responsibility initiatives that extend beyond profit generation. They invest in community development, support charitable causes, and actively contribute to positive change.

Imagine an electronics company that donates a portion of its profits to local schools to promote STEM education. By engaging in meaningful social responsibility, the brand fosters goodwill and loyalty within its community.

Environmental Stewardship and Sustainability

Ethical brands embrace environmental stewardship and sustainable practices. Businesses that prioritize reducing their ecological footprint, using renewable resources, and minimizing waste resonate with environmentally conscious consumers.

Consider a beauty brand that uses recyclable packaging and sources ingredients from sustainable farms. Ethical commitment to sustainability aligns with consumer values and attracts a loyal customer base.

Empathy and Consumer-Centricity

Ethical brands display empathy and prioritize consumer needs. Businesses that actively listen to customer feedback, address concerns, and adapt to changing preferences demonstrate consumer-centricity.

Imagine a tech company that designs products based on user needs and preferences, providing customer support that exceeds expectations. This empathetic approach builds lasting relationships and fosters customer loyalty.

Long-Term Relationships and Loyalty

Ethical brands invest in building long-term relationships with customers. By consistently delivering quality, ethical practices, and positive experiences, brands can foster customer loyalty that transcends transactional interactions.

Consider a financial institution that offers personalized financial planning and advice to help customers achieve their goals. Through these ongoing relationships, the brand earns trust and loyalty as customers witness the brand's commitment to their financial well-being.

Employee Well-being and Ethical Culture

Ethical brands prioritize employee well-being and cultivate an ethical company culture. Businesses that treat employees with respect, provide fair compensation, and promote diversity and inclusion create an ethical ecosystem that resonates with consumers.

Imagine a software company that offers flexible work arrangements, values employee input, and supports professional development. Ethical treatment of employees extends to ethical branding, as consumers align with brands that prioritize their workforce's well-being.

Consistency and Reliability

Ethical brands embody consistency and reliability. By consistently upholding ethical values and delivering on promises, brands build a reputation for dependability that resonates with consumers.

Consider an energy company that consistently invests in renewable energy projects and supports conservation efforts. This commitment to consistency aligns with consumer expectations and reinforces the brand's ethical image.

Ethical brands that prioritize trust and loyalty as

accelerators create a positive cycle of success. By building authentic connections with consumers through transparency, responsibility, and ethical actions, these brands foster loyalty, inspire positive word-of-mouth, and contribute to a better world. Trust and loyalty become the driving forces that propel ethical brands to greater heights, solidifying their place as responsible and impactful market leaders.

Real-Life Case: The Body Shop's Ethical Success

Background: The Body Shop is a global cosmetics and skincare brand founded by Anita Roddick in 1976. The company is renowned for its commitment to ethical business practices, social responsibility, and sustainability.

The Situation: Anita Roddick started The Body Shop with the aim of creating a business that aligned with her values and promoted positive change. She believed in using business as a force for good and focused on selling natural, cruelty-free beauty products.

Ethical Business Practices: The Body Shop's commitment to ethical business practices was evident in various aspects of its operations:

Ethical Sourcing: The company pioneered the concept of ethical sourcing by using sustainably sourced ingredients and working directly with communities that provided raw materials.

Cruelty-Free: The Body Shop was one of the first companies to adopt a strict policy against animal testing. This stance resonated with consumers who valued cruelty-free products.

Fair Trade: The Body Shop sourced ingredients such as shea butter and cocoa butter from fair trade cooperatives, ensuring that producers received fair compensation for their work.

Environmental Stewardship: The company worked to reduce

its environmental impact by using eco-friendly packaging, promoting recycling, and minimizing waste.

Positive Impact: The Body Shop's ethical business practices not only resonated with consumers but also contributed to its success. The company's commitment to social and environmental responsibility created a loyal customer base that admired its values.

The Body Shop's impact extended beyond its products. The company's campaigns on issues like animal testing, domestic violence, and environmental protection brought attention to important social and ethical issues.

Acquisition by Natura &Co: In 2017, The Body Shop was acquired by Natura &Co, a Brazilian company known for its commitment to sustainability. This acquisition marked the joining of two companies with shared values, further cementing The Body Shop's legacy of ethical success.

Key Takeaways:

Ethical Values as a Business Foundation: The Body Shop's success was built on a foundation of ethical values, which resonated with consumers and set it apart from competitors.

Holistic Approach to Ethics: The company addressed multiple ethical aspects, from animal testing to fair trade and environmental sustainability.

Loyalty and Impact: Ethical success can lead to customer loyalty, positive brand perception, and the ability to make a significant impact on societal issues.

The Body Shop's journey of ethical success exemplifies how a commitment to ethical values and practices can drive business success, create a positive impact, and inspire a sense of purpose that goes beyond profit.

CHAPTER 10

Ethics in the Digital Age

"In the digital world, transparency and integrity must be the core values that guide professional behaviour. Organisations must use data in responsible and ethical ways."

- Dave Yardley

Navigating the Ethical Landscape

T he digital age has ushered in a new era of technological advancement and connectivity, transforming the way we live, work, and interact. Amidst the rapid pace of innovation, the need for ethical considerations has become more critical than ever before. Ethics in the digital age encompasses a range of complex challenges and opportunities, spanning from data privacy and artificial intelligence to online behavior and digital responsibility. Navigating this ethical landscape is essential to ensure that the benefits of technology are harnessed for the greater good while avoiding unintended negative consequences.

Data Privacy and Security

In the digital age, the collection and utilization of personal data have become commonplace. Ethical concerns arise regarding the protection of individuals' privacy and the responsible handling of their sensitive information.

Imagine a social media platform that implements strict data encryption measures, informs users about data usage, and offers transparent opt-out options. Ethical data practices ensure that users' privacy is respected, fostering trust in digital interactions.

Artificial Intelligence and Automation

The rise of artificial intelligence (AI) and automation presents ethical challenges related to accountability, fairness, and transparency. Decisions made by AI algorithms can impact individuals' lives, and ensuring these decisions align with ethical principles is crucial.

Consider an AI-driven hiring tool that eliminates human bias in the selection process. Ethical AI integration involves continuous monitoring and adjusting algorithms to prevent discriminatory outcomes.

Digital Inclusivity and Accessibility

The digital age has the potential to either exacerbate or alleviate societal inequalities. Ethical considerations encompass making digital platforms accessible to all individuals, regardless of their physical abilities or socio-economic status.

Imagine a website that adheres to accessibility guidelines, ensuring that people with disabilities can navigate and interact with its content. Ethical digital inclusivity reflects a commitment to equal participation in the digital realm.

Cybersecurity and Responsible Use

Ethical practices in the digital age extend to cybersecurity and responsible digital behavior. Protecting digital systems from cyber threats and ensuring that individuals use technology ethically are essential components of digital ethics.

Consider an organization that educates its employees about

phishing scams and cyber hygiene, promoting responsible online behavior. Ethical cybersecurity practices safeguard individuals' digital well-being and prevent harm.

Misinformation and Digital Literacy

The digital age has seen the proliferation of misinformation and fake news, raising concerns about the manipulation of public discourse. Ethical digital literacy initiatives aim to educate individuals about critically evaluating information and discerning credible sources.

Imagine an educational campaign that teaches students how to verify information before sharing it online. Ethical digital literacy empowers individuals to be responsible consumers and sharers of information.

Online Behavior and Digital Citizenship

Ethical online behavior is essential for fostering a positive digital culture. Digital citizenship involves treating others with respect, practicing empathy, and contributing constructively to online discussions.

Consider an online community that enforces guidelines against hate speech and promotes civil discourse. Ethical online behavior contributes to a safe and inclusive digital environment for all users.

Environmental Impact of Technology

The digital age's rapid growth is accompanied by concerns about its environmental impact. Ethical considerations involve developing sustainable technologies, minimizing electronic waste, and reducing energy consumption.

Imagine a tech company that designs energy-efficient devices and promotes e-waste recycling programs. Ethical technology development takes into account the long-term environmental consequences of digital advancements.

Accountability for Algorithmic Decisions

Algorithms drive many digital processes, from search engine results to social media feeds. Ensuring transparency, accountability, and fairness in algorithmic decisions is an ethical imperative.

Consider an e-commerce platform that discloses how its recommendation algorithm works and allows users to adjust their preferences. Ethical algorithmic practices prioritize user understanding and control.

Ethics in the digital age requires a collective effort from individuals, organizations, policymakers, and technology developers. By upholding ethical principles in the design, implementation, and use of digital technologies, we can harness the potential of the digital age while safeguarding individual rights, promoting equality, and creating a more just and responsible digital society.

Navigating Digital Ethics: Responsibility in Technology and Social Media

In today's interconnected world, technology and social media have transformed how we communicate, access information, and interact with the world around us. However, with the benefits of digital innovation come ethical challenges that require careful consideration and responsible behavior. Navigating digital ethics involves understanding the implications of our online actions, upholding values in the virtual realm, and ensuring that technology and social media contribute positively to society.

Ethical Use of Data

One of the most pressing issues in digital ethics is the ethical use of data. Personal information is collected, stored, and analyzed by various digital platforms, raising concerns about privacy, consent, and data security.

Imagine a tech company that anonymizes and protects user data, allowing individuals to control how their information is used. Ethical data practices prioritize user consent, transparency, and safeguarding sensitive information.

Digital Responsibility

Digital responsibility involves recognizing the impact of our online actions on ourselves and others. It encompasses refraining from cyberbullying, practicing empathy in online interactions, and promoting a positive digital environment.

Consider an educational campaign that encourages users to think twice before sharing hurtful comments or false information online. Ethical digital responsibility fosters a culture of kindness and respect in the digital realm.

Algorithmic Transparency

The algorithms that power social media platforms and search engines influence the information we see. Ethical considerations involve ensuring algorithmic transparency, avoiding biased outcomes, and providing users with control over their online experience.

Imagine a social media platform that allows users to customize their content preferences and understand how algorithms curate their feeds. Ethical algorithmic transparency empowers users to shape their digital engagement.

Combating Misinformation

The spread of misinformation and fake news poses ethical challenges in the digital age. Ethical behavior entails verifying information before sharing, promoting critical thinking, and being aware of the potential impact of false information.

Consider a fact-checking organization that works to debunk false claims and educate the public about reliable sources. Ethical efforts to combat misinformation contribute to a more informed and responsible digital society.

Balancing Online and Offline Life

Ethical digital behavior involves finding a balance between online and offline life. Excessive screen time, digital addiction, and neglecting in-person relationships can have negative consequences on mental health and overall well-being.

Imagine a digital wellness campaign that encourages individuals to set boundaries for screen time and engage in meaningful face-to-face interactions. Ethical digital behavior prioritizes holistic well-being over constant digital engagement.

Addressing Cybersecurity Concerns

Cybersecurity is a central ethical concern in the digital age. Protecting sensitive information, preventing data breaches, and ensuring the security of digital systems are vital components of responsible digital behavior.

Consider an organization that invests in robust cybersecurity measures, undergoes regular security audits, and educates employees about online threats. Ethical cybersecurity practices safeguard individuals and organizations from potential harm.

Promoting Inclusivity and Accessibility

Digital ethics also encompass promoting inclusivity and accessibility. Ensuring that digital platforms are designed to accommodate individuals with disabilities and diverse backgrounds is essential for equal participation in the digital world.

Imagine a website that adheres to web accessibility guidelines, making it usable for individuals with visual impairments or mobility challenges. Ethical digital design ensures that everyone can access and engage with online content.

Digital Footprint and Privacy

Individuals leave a digital footprint through their online activities, from social media posts to online purchases. Ethical behavior involves considering the potential long-term consequences of digital actions and protecting personal privacy. One must be conscious of the fact that what you do on the internet stays on the internet, even long after you have forgotten about it.

Consider a digital literacy program that educates young people about the permanence of online content and the importance of managing their digital footprint. Ethical digital citizenship involves responsible online self-presentation and decision-making.

Navigating digital ethics requires a collective effort to ensure that technology and social media enhance our lives rather than compromise our values. By making informed, ethical choices in our digital interactions, we can contribute to a more responsible, respectful, and inclusive online environment that benefits individuals and society as a whole.

Digital Citizenship: Ethical Behavior in Online Communities

As our lives become increasingly intertwined with the digital world, the concept of digital citizenship has emerged as a crucial framework for promoting ethical behavior, responsible engagement, and positive interactions in online communities. Just as good citizenship involves respecting laws, contributing to society, and treating others with respect in the physical world, digital citizenship extends these principles to the virtual realm. Upholding ethical behavior in online communities is not only a personal responsibility but also a collective effort to create a safe, inclusive, and constructive digital environment.

Respectful Online Communication

Ethical digital citizens engage in respectful online communication. This involves treating others with kindness, empathy, and civility, even in the face of differing opinions.

Imagine an online discussion forum where participants engage in thoughtful debates without resorting to personal attacks. Ethical behavior in online communication fosters an environment where diverse viewpoints can be shared without fear of hostility.

Critical Thinking and Information Evaluation

Ethical digital citizens practice critical thinking when consuming and sharing information online. They verify the accuracy of information before sharing it and avoid spreading misinformation or fake news.

Consider an individual who fact-checks news articles and cross-references sources before sharing information on social media. Ethical digital citizens contribute to the dissemination of reliable and accurate information.

Responsible Digital Footprint

Digital citizens are mindful of their online presence and the impact of their digital actions. They manage their digital footprint by considering the potential long-term consequences of their online activities.

Imagine a student who is cautious about the content they post on social media to ensure that it aligns with their future goals and values. Ethical digital citizens understand that their online activities can have implications beyond the immediate moment.

Respecting Privacy and Consent

Ethical digital citizens respect others' privacy and obtain consent before sharing personal information or images. They understand the importance of protecting individuals' right to control their online presence.

Consider a blogger who seeks permission before using photos of others in their online posts. Ethical behavior in respecting privacy fosters trust and a sense of safety in online interactions.

Combating Cyberbullying and Harassment

Ethical digital citizens take a stand against cyberbullying and harassment. They intervene when they witness such behavior, and they strive to create online environments where individuals can express themselves without fear.

Imagine a social media user who reports instances of cyberbullying and supports the target of the bullying with words of encouragement. Ethical behavior in addressing cyberbullying contributes to a more compassionate and inclusive digital landscape.

Positive Contribution to Online Communities

Digital citizens actively contribute positively to online communities. They engage in meaningful discussions, share valuable insights, and help create an atmosphere of collaboration and learning.

Consider an online forum member who regularly provides well-researched answers to questions and offers support to newcomers. Ethical digital citizens enhance the quality of online communities through their positive contributions.

Empathy and Inclusivity

Ethical digital citizens practice empathy and inclusivity in their online interactions. They consider the feelings and perspectives of others, working to create online spaces that are welcoming to individuals from diverse backgrounds.

Imagine a gaming community that promotes an inclusive environment by actively discouraging derogatory language and behaviors. Ethical behavior in promoting empathy and inclusivity helps counteract online toxicity.

Educating Others and Promoting Digital Literacy

Digital citizens take on the responsibility of educating others about ethical online behavior and digital literacy. They help others navigate the digital landscape safely and responsibly.

Consider an educator who teaches students about online privacy, proper citation, and the importance of respecting intellectual property. Ethical digital citizens actively contribute to raising awareness and promoting responsible digital practices.

By embracing the principles of digital citizenship and practicing ethical behavior in online communities, individuals collectively shape the nature of the digital world. Just as in the physical world, ethical behavior contributes to a more harmonious, respectful, and constructive online environment that benefits everyone involved.

Real-Life Case: Apple's Stand for User Privacy

Background: Apple Inc., a technology giant known for its innovative products, has been a prominent advocate for user privacy and ethical practices in the digital age.

The Situation: In recent years, concerns about digital privacy and data security have become increasingly relevant due to the widespread collection and misuse of user data by various tech companies. As data breaches and privacy scandals made headlines, Apple took a strong stand on protecting user information.

Ethical Approach to Privacy: Apple's commitment to user

privacy is evident in several key decisions and actions:

Encryption: Apple implemented end-to-end encryption for iMessage and FaceTime, making it extremely difficult for unauthorized parties, including the company itself, to access user messages and calls.

App Tracking Transparency: In 2021, Apple introduced the App Tracking Transparency feature, requiring app developers to obtain user consent before tracking their activities across other apps and websites.

Privacy Labels: Apple introduced privacy labels on the App Store, providing users with clear information about how apps collect and use their data before they download them.

Differential Privacy: Apple uses differential privacy techniques to collect aggregated data from users without compromising individual privacy.

Balancing Innovation and Privacy: Apple's stance on privacy has sometimes led to conflicts with other tech companies and advertisers. For instance, the company's decision to restrict third-party cookies and limit tracking mechanisms sparked debates about the balance between user privacy and targeted advertising.

Consumer Trust and Ethical Reputation: Apple's ethical approach to privacy has resonated with consumers who value their digital rights and data security. The company's commitment to transparency and giving users control over their data has contributed to its reputation as a tech company that prioritizes ethics.

Key Takeaways:

Privacy as a Priority: Apple's commitment to user privacy showcases how ethics can guide decisions in the digital age, even in a highly competitive tech industry.

<u>Transparency and Consent:</u> Ethical practices involve clear communication, informed consent, and giving users control over their data.

<u>Balancing Interests:</u> Ethical decisions often involve balancing user rights with technological innovation and industry norms.

Apple's case demonstrates how a tech company can navigate the complexities of the digital age by placing ethical considerations at the forefront of its decisions. By prioritizing user privacy and data security, Apple has set an example for the industry and highlighted the importance of ethical practices in the digital realm.

CHAPTER 11

The Global Impact of Ethics

"We need to evolve and articulate a global ethics for a global civilization that integrates and evolves the passionate truths of every great system of knowledge - pre-modern, modern, and post-modern"

- Marc Gafni

Shaping a Better World

Ethics, the moral principles that guide human behavior, have a profound impact that transcends borders and cultures, shaping the way societies function and interact on a global scale. As the world becomes increasingly interconnected, the importance of ethics in influencing social, economic, and environmental dynamics becomes more evident. The global impact of ethics extends across various domains, from international relations and business practices to environmental stewardship and humanitarian efforts.

Promoting Peace and Diplomacy

Ethics play a significant role in international relations and diplomacy. Ethical considerations guide negotiations, conflict resolution, and efforts to maintain global peace. Nations that prioritize diplomacy and ethical engagement foster a more stable and cooperative international environment.

Imagine diplomatic efforts to address global challenges, such as climate change or disarmament, driven by ethical considerations for the well-being of all nations and future generations. Ethical diplomacy contributes to a more just and peaceful world.

Fostering Human Rights and Social Justice

Ethical values underpin the pursuit of human rights and social justice around the world. Global movements for equality, inclusivity, and the elimination of discrimination are fueled by the ethical belief in the inherent dignity and worth of every individual.

Consider human rights organizations working tirelessly to advocate for marginalized communities and hold violators accountable. Ethical commitments to social justice drive positive change and amplify the voices of those who are oppressed.

Global Business Ethics

Ethics in business transcends national boundaries, influencing the conduct of multinational corporations and shaping the global economy. Businesses that uphold ethical principles in their operations, supply chains, and interactions with stakeholders contribute to sustainable economic growth and responsible resource management. This has been one of the major failings of most western businesses in Africa, especially the oil exploration and mining companies. They exploit the people, create political instability, destroy the environment and impoverish the populace.

Imagine a global corporation that ensures fair wages for workers across different countries, adheres to environmental standards, and supports local communities. Ethical business practices promote positive economic and social impacts on a global scale.

Environmental Stewardship

The global impact of ethics is particularly evident in environmental stewardship. Ethical considerations surrounding climate change, pollution, and resource depletion emphasize the responsibility to protect the planet for current and future generations.

Consider international agreements and initiatives aimed at addressing climate change, driven by ethical commitments to preserving the environment. Ethical environmental stewardship promotes the well-being of both humanity and the planet.

Cross-Cultural Dialogue and Understanding

Ethics foster cross-cultural dialogue and understanding, bridging cultural divides and promoting mutual respect. Recognizing and appreciating diverse ethical perspectives enhances global cooperation and empathy among nations and individuals. The evidence of this can be seen in the western push for African adoption of Western model of democratic system of government. It completely ignores, and in most cases denigrates existing indigenous political systems, thereby breeding a dysfunctional political culture.

Imagine cultural exchanges that promote open conversations about ethical values, leading to increased understanding and collaboration among people from different backgrounds. Ethical dialogue nurtures a sense of interconnectedness among all humanity.

Humanitarian Efforts

Humanitarian initiatives are deeply rooted in ethical principles of compassion, empathy, and solidarity. Global organizations and individuals dedicated to providing aid and relief in times of crisis demonstrate the global impact of ethical values in action.

Consider emergency response teams providing assistance to communities affected by natural disasters or conflicts. Ethical humanitarian efforts prioritize human well-being and alleviate suffering on a global scale.

Digital and Technological Ethics

As technology shapes our interconnected world, digital and technological ethics play a crucial role in safeguarding individual rights, privacy, and equitable access to information. Ethical considerations guide the responsible development and use of technology for the betterment of society.

Imagine international agreements and regulations that address digital privacy and data protection, promoting ethical use of technology across borders. Ethical digital practices ensure that technological advancements benefit humanity without compromising fundamental rights.

Shared Global Responsibility

The global impact of ethics is a reminder of the shared responsibility that humanity bears toward one another and the planet. Ethical values have the power to transcend cultural, political, and geographical boundaries, uniting us in our quest for a more just, equitable, and sustainable world.

As we collectively navigate the complex challenges of our interconnected world, embracing ethical principles can guide our decisions and actions toward creating a global society that respects human dignity, protects the environment, and works together to shape a better future for all.

Cultural Sensitivity: Navigating Ethics Across Borders

In a world characterized by diverse cultures, values, and perspectives, cultural sensitivity has become an essential component of ethical behavior. Navigating ethics across borders requires a deep understanding and respect for cultural differences, ensuring that our actions and decisions align with the values and norms of the societies we interact with. Cultural sensitivity fosters positive interactions, avoids misunderstandings, and upholds the universal principles of respect and empathy. This was not the case in the colonial activities in Africa. While there was a general attempt to demonize the indigenous cultures, France went even further with a policy to wipe away the existing cultures in their colonial domains and assimilate the people into the french culture.

Understanding Cultural Context

Cultural sensitivity begins with an effort to understand the cultural context in which interactions take place. Recognizing the historical, social, and cultural factors that shape a society's values is essential for making informed ethical choices.

Imagine a business expanding its operations to a new country and taking the time to learn about local customs, traditions, and business practices. Cultural sensitivity helps prevent unintentional cultural faux pas and promotes respectful engagement.

Respecting Different Norms

Cultural sensitivity involves recognizing that ethical norms can vary significantly from one culture to another. What is considered ethical in one society may not hold the same significance in another. Respecting and adapting to different ethical norms demonstrates openness and inclusivity.

Consider a healthcare provider working in a multicultural environment, where understanding patients' cultural beliefs about medical treatments is crucial for providing respectful care. Cultural sensitivity ensures that patients' values are respected while delivering appropriate healthcare services.

Communication and Language

Effective communication is at the core of cultural

sensitivity. Being mindful of language barriers and adapting communication styles to accommodate different cultural preferences promotes understanding and minimizes misinterpretation.

Imagine a global team collaborating on a project using a shared language, while also making an effort to provide translations or explanations for cultural idioms. Cultural sensitivity ensures that everyone is on the same page and can contribute effectively.

Balancing Universal Ethics with Cultural Nuances

Cultural sensitivity doesn't imply that ethical standards should be compromised. While cultural differences are respected, there are universal ethical principles that transcend cultural boundaries, such as honesty, respect for human dignity, and fairness.

Consider a multinational organization that adheres to international labor standards and human rights principles while also respecting cultural practices that don't violate these universal ethical values. Balancing universal ethics with cultural nuances requires a thoughtful approach.

Avoiding Cultural Stereotypes

Cultural sensitivity means avoiding generalizations and stereotypes about a particular culture. Recognizing that individuals within a culture are diverse and have unique experiences helps prevent unfair judgments and assumptions.

Imagine an educator who refrains from assigning certain roles to students based on cultural stereotypes. Cultural sensitivity fosters an environment where every individual's abilities and aspirations are respected.

Promoting Inclusivity

Cultural sensitivity promotes inclusivity by creating

environments where individuals from various cultural backgrounds feel valued and accepted. It involves creating spaces where diverse perspectives are encouraged and celebrated.

Consider an international conference that actively seeks speakers from different regions to ensure a diverse range of viewpoints. Cultural sensitivity enriches discussions and promotes a more comprehensive understanding of complex issues.

Continuous Learning and Adaptation

Cultural sensitivity is an ongoing process that requires a willingness to learn and adapt. As cultures evolve and interactions become more global, staying informed about cultural changes and shifts is essential for maintaining ethical conduct.

Imagine an expatriate employee who regularly participates in cultural sensitivity training to stay attuned to cultural shifts in their host country. Cultural sensitivity involves a commitment to continuous learning.

Cultural Diplomacy

Cultural sensitivity contributes to cultural diplomacy, fostering positive international relations and mutual understanding between nations. By respecting and valuing each other's cultural differences, countries can engage in diplomatic efforts that bridge divides and promote peace.

Imagine cultural exchange programs that facilitate understanding between nations through art, music, and literature. Cultural sensitivity enhances the potential for productive international collaboration.

Cultural sensitivity is a cornerstone of ethical behavior in a diverse and interconnected world. It promotes respectful engagement, understanding, and empathy across borders, ultimately contributing to a more harmonious and inclusive global community.

Ethical Global Citizenship: Success Beyond National Boundaries

In an era of increasing globalization and interconnectedness, the concept of ethical global citizenship has gained prominence as individuals, organizations, and nations recognize the importance of taking responsibility for actions that transcend national borders. Ethical global citizenship extends beyond local concerns and challenges us to consider the impact of our decisions on a global scale. It involves embracing ethical values that promote cooperation, sustainability, and social responsibility, ultimately contributing to a more just and interconnected world.

Embracing Interconnectedness

Ethical global citizenship begins with recognizing that our actions are not confined by geographical boundaries. In an interconnected world, decisions made in one part of the globe can have far-reaching consequences for people, communities, and environments worldwide.

Imagine a fashion brand that sources materials from different countries. Ethical global citizenship prompts the brand to ensure that the production processes adhere to fair labor practices and environmental sustainability, regardless of where they occur.

Promoting Social Responsibility

Ethical global citizens take responsibility for addressing social issues that extend beyond their immediate surroundings. This may involve supporting global efforts to eradicate poverty, promote education, or ensure access to clean water.

Consider a nonprofit organization that provides educational

resources to underserved communities in developing countries. Ethical global citizenship involves recognizing a shared responsibility for creating a more equitable world.

Environmental Stewardship

The impact of environmental decisions knows no borders. Ethical global citizens understand the urgency of addressing climate change, preserving biodiversity, and promoting sustainable practices for the well-being of the planet and future generations.

Imagine an energy company that invests in renewable energy projects in multiple countries. Ethical global citizenship involves prioritizing sustainable energy solutions that transcend national interests.

Supporting Human Rights

Ethical global citizens advocate for the protection of human rights everywhere. This includes standing up against violations, discrimination, and oppression regardless of where they occur. Contrary to acceptable universal ethical standards, the US has been complicit in the violation of human rights in the Middle East and other places in Africa under the pretence of policing the world.

Consider individuals who participate in human rights campaigns to raise awareness about issues like child labor or gender inequality. Ethical global citizenship involves acknowledging that human rights are universal and indivisible.

Contributing to Global Peace

Ethical global citizenship is intertwined with efforts to promote global peace and security. Individuals and nations that prioritize diplomacy, conflict resolution, and disarmament contribute to a safer and more harmonious world. While projecting an image, through the mainstream media, as a beacon of uprightness in the world, the United States of America in particular, has been guilty of sponsoring armed struggle, insurrection and political changes in many countries of the world.

Imagine international negotiations aimed at preventing conflicts and reducing the threat of nuclear weapons. Ethical global citizenship requires a commitment to working collaboratively for the collective well-being.

Respecting Cultural Diversity

Ethical global citizenship entails respecting and valuing cultural diversity around the world. It involves recognizing the richness that different cultures bring to the global community and avoiding cultural imperialism.

Consider a traveler who engages with local communities and learns about their traditions and customs. Ethical global citizenship promotes cross-cultural understanding and appreciates the uniqueness of every culture.

Acting Locally and Globally

Ethical global citizenship doesn't negate the importance of local action. Instead, it emphasizes that the choices we make locally can have global repercussions. By acting ethically at both levels, we contribute to a more ethical and interconnected world.

Imagine a business that supports local artisans while also ensuring that its supply chain aligns with fair trade practices. Ethical global citizenship recognizes the interconnectedness of local and global economies.

Engaging in Global Initiatives

Ethical global citizenship involves active engagement in global initiatives, whether through supporting international organizations, participating in humanitarian efforts, or advocating for policy changes that benefit the global community.

Consider individuals who volunteer for global health organizations or advocate for sustainable development goals. Ethical global citizenship means actively contributing to initiatives that address global challenges.

Ethical global citizenship transcends national boundaries, reminding us of our shared humanity and the collective responsibility to create a better world for all. By embracing ethical values that promote cooperation, social responsibility, and environmental sustainability, we can contribute to a more just, equitable, and interconnected global community.

Real-Life Case: The United Nations Universal Declaration of Human Rights

Background: The Universal Declaration of Human Rights (UDHR) is a landmark document adopted by the United Nations (UN) General Assembly in 1948. It is a global example of the impact of ethics on human rights, freedom, and dignity.

The Situation: In the aftermath of World War II, the international community sought to prevent future atrocities and establish a foundation for universal human rights. The UDHR was drafted as a response to the widespread human rights abuses that occurred during the war.

Ethical Foundation: The UDHR is rooted in the ethical principles of human dignity, equality, and fundamental freedoms. It asserts that all individuals, regardless of their background, are entitled to certain inherent rights and liberties.

Global Impact: The UDHR's global impact is profound and far-reaching:

Basis for International Law: The UDHR laid the groundwork for subsequent international human rights treaties and conventions. It became a foundation for modern international human rights law.

Inspiration for Constitutions: The UDHR has served as a source of inspiration for the development of national constitutions around the world, influencing legal frameworks that protect human rights.

Advocacy and Accountability: The UDHR provides a universal standard against which governments and organizations can be held accountable for human rights violations.

Social and Political Movements: The UDHR has been a powerful tool for activists and advocates working to address issues such as gender inequality, racial discrimination, and the rights of marginalized groups.

Long-Term Impact: The UDHR's principles have contributed to shaping a more just and equitable world, promoting the idea that every person deserves to live with dignity and respect. It has fostered international dialogue on human rights and continues to serve as a moral compass for addressing global challenges.

Key Takeaways:

Ethics and Human Rights: The UDHR illustrates how ethical principles can drive the creation of global standards for human rights and justice.

Global Relevance: Ethical documents like the UDHR can transcend cultural and national boundaries, influencing laws, policies, and attitudes worldwide.

Long-Term Vision: The UDHR's impact demonstrates the enduring influence of ethical principles on shaping a more equitable and compassionate world.

The Universal Declaration of Human Rights stands as a real-life case study of how ethics can have a profound and lasting impact on a global scale, shaping legal frameworks, inspiring social change, and promoting the dignity and rights of all individuals.

CONCLUSION

Reflecting on Ethical Success - A Pathway to Lasting Achievement

As we journey through the multifaceted landscape of success, we inevitably encounter the compass of ethics guiding our way. The exploration of ethics in the pursuit of success is not just a theoretical endeavor; it is a practical roadmap that can steer us toward a more meaningful and enduring achievement. From the realms of personal growth and leadership to the intricacies of digital interactions and global citizenship, the tapestry of ethical success weaves together a narrative of integrity, empathy, and responsible action.

Ethics, as a guiding principle, offers us the assurance that true success extends beyond mere accomplishments. It encompasses the alignment of our actions with our core values, fostering a sense of purpose that transcends short-term gains. It's not about just reaching the destination, but about the journey we undertake and the legacy we leave behind.

In our exploration, we have delved into the foundations of ethical success, recognizing the significance of integrity as the bedrock upon which lasting achievement is built. We have navigated through intricate ethical dilemmas, harnessed the power of authenticity, and harnessed the force of ethical innovation and creativity. We have understood that ethical success is not confined to individual endeavors; it extends to businesses, digital interactions, and global consciousness.

From personal growth to responsible global citizenship, ethical success calls us to embrace a higher standard of achievement —one that resonates with our values, contributes positively to society, and leaves a mark that endures across generations. It is about integrating ethics into the fabric of our decisions, shaping a legacy that reflects our commitment to the betterment of ourselves and the world around us.

As we reflect on this journey through the pages of ethical success, may we carry forward the wisdom gained and the principles explored. Let us embark on our endeavors with a renewed sense of purpose, infusing our actions with ethical considerations that elevate our pursuit of success. Let the guiding star of integrity illuminate our paths, ensuring that every step we take is not only one of accomplishment but also one of ethical fulfillment.

Ultimately, the voyage of ethical success is not just about the goals we achieve but the values we uphold, not just about the accolades we receive but the impact we make. With ethics as our compass, we navigate the waters of success with unwavering integrity, setting sail toward a horizon of achievement that is both meaningful and enduring.

REFERENCES FOR FURTHER READING

Here are some authors and their notable books related to key concepts of ethics:

Virtue Ethics:

1. Alasdair MacIntyre: Author of "After Virtue: A Study in Moral Theory"
2. Julia Annas: Author of "Intelligent Virtue"
3. Rosalind Hursthouse: Author of "On Virtue Ethics"

Utilitarianism:

4. John Stuart Mill: Author of "Utilitarianism"
5. Peter Singer: Author of "Practical Ethics"
6. Jeremy Bentham: Author of "An Introduction to the Principles of Morals and Legislation"

Deontology:

7. Immanuel Kant: Author of "Groundwork for the Metaphysics of Morals"
8. Christine Korsgaard: Author of "The Sources of Normativity"
9. Onora O'Neill: Author of "Constructions of Reason: Explorations of Kant's Practical Philosophy"

Ethical Dilemmas:

10. Kwame Anthony Appiah: Author of "The Ethics of Identity"
11. Michael J. Sandel: Author of "Justice: What's the Right Thing to Do?"
12. Harry Gensler: Author of "Ethics and the Golden Rule"

Corporate Social Responsibility (CSR):

13. Archie B. Carroll: Author of "Business Ethics and Corporate Social Responsibility: A Brief History"
14. Milton Friedman: Author of "Capitalism and Freedom" (discusses CSR from a different perspective)

15. Norman E. Bowie: Author of "Business Ethics: A Kantian Perspective"

Stakeholder Theory:

16. R. Edward Freeman: Author of "Stakeholder Theory: The State of the Art"
17. Thomas Donaldson and Lee E. Preston: Authors of "The Stakeholder Theory of the Corporation"
18. Edward S. Sanford: Author of "The Corporation as Social Contract"

Here are some authors who have written books that align with the themes in this book.

Ethical Leadership:

19. John C. Maxwell: Author of "Ethics 101: What Every Leader Needs To Know"
20. Bill George: Author of "True North: Discover Your Authentic Leadership"

Integrity and Trust:

21. Stephen M.R. Covey: Author of "The Speed of Trust: The One Thing That Changes Everything"
22. Warren Bennis: Author of "An Invented Life: Reflections on Leadership and Change"

Empathy and Collaboration:

23. Adam Grant: Author of "Give and Take: Why Helping Others Drives Our Success"
24. Simon Sinek: Author of "Leaders Eat Last: Why Some Teams Pull Together and Others Don't"

Decision-Making:

25. Chip Heath and Dan Heath: Authors of "Decisive: How to Make Better Choices in Life and Work"
26. Michael J. Sandel: Author of "What Money Can't Buy: The Moral Limits of Markets"

Sustainability:

27. Ray Anderson: Author of "Business Lessons from a Radical Industrialist"
28. Daniel C. Esty and Andrew S. Winston: Authors of "Green to Gold: How Smart Companies Use Environmental Strategy to Innovate, Create Value, and Build Competitive Advantage"

Communication Ethics:

29. Deborah Tannen: Author of "The Argument Culture: Moving from Debate to Dialogue"
30. John A. Daly: Author of "Advocacy: Championing Ideas and Influencing Others"

Innovation and Creativity:

31. Tim Brown: Author of "Change by Design: How Design Thinking Transforms Organizations and Inspires Innovation"
32. Ed Catmull: Author of "Creativity, Inc.: Overcoming the Unseen Forces That Stand in the Way of True Inspiration"

ABOUT THE AUTHOR

Victor Olewunne

Victor Olewunne is the Chief Consultant at Protarget Communications Limited. He has been in the marketing communication profession for over 30 years. Yes, 30 years of research, business consultancy and marketing communication challenges. Since compassion and empathy is at the core of his person, he has learnt to dig deep, filter out the noises and analytically identify what the real life's problems are. That done, the solution he proffers become  fun that turns everything around for good. His experience as a life and business coach has taught him that there are more perceived problems than real ones. With the right information and tools, no problem is worth a sleepless night.Through his entrepreneurship journey, starting and running several businesses over the years, he has come across and surmounted most of the challenges of life and business. His life's focus now is to extend his experience, researched and proven solutions to all those who may be at one of the cross roads of life.He is here to hold your hand to a life of powerful information and solutions.

Victor Olewunne. BA. MPE (Masters in Professional Ethics)

BOOKS BY THIS AUTHOR

Easy Steps To Make Your Child Top The Class.

The Secret of High Performance Students Revealed.This book guides parents on what they can and need to do to greatly improve the academic performance of their child in school. It includes the role of the parents and that of the child.

Discover Your Child's Talent, For Early Success In Life.

This book guides parents on how to discover and nurture the child's talent, towards pursuing a profession aligned to their natural talent early in life. The child thus, follows a passion and achieves an early success in life.

Deontological Examination Of The Ethics Of The Knowledge Economy

This book examines the place of duty ethics in globalisation. It is about the application of duty ethics in the knowledge economy. In this era globalisation, the world is called to pay closer attention to the duty we owe each other, the ethics that makes the world a better place to live in.

What Women Want In A Man, To Secure Her Admiration And Enduring Love

Men are often at a loss about what women really want, or what they can do to consistently please the women in their life. This book reveals most of those things that matter with women when it come to relationship with the opposite sex. A man who is privileged to read this book will find it really easy to secure, for the long term, the love and admiration of his woman.

Opportunity Unleashed: The Ultimate Guide To Discovering, Creating And Maximising Success

Opportunity Unleashed" is a transformative guide that illuminates the path to success by empowering readers to harness the full potential of opportunities in every aspect of their lives. This comprehensive book takes readers on a journey of self-discovery, creative thinking, and strategic planning to seize opportunities and turn them into remarkable achievements. From business ventures to personal growth, this guide equips readers with the mindset, skills, and actionable steps needed to unleash their true potential and create a life of fulfillment and success.

Your Tyre Or Your Life.

This book reveals the risk we run when we neglect the air pressure of our vehicle tyres. It shows how close monitoring and maintenance of vehicle tyres can save your life and that of your family.

Mothers Work Life Balance: The 25 Ways To Get It Right

In this era when most women work, one of their greatest challenge is how to balance being a good mother and a wife, and at same time be a well bred professional in her place of work. This book helps all women in this dilemma to navigate the challenges.

Make A Man Love You For Life: The Secret Of Men's Love Revealed.

Women naturally fret about the one thing that matters most to them in a relationship, the love of their partner. To address such anxiety, this book provides a solution that calms the nerves of any woman in a relationship. It tells in a very simple way what keeps men loving their women. Follow the guide and see the magic.

Dealing With Workplace Hostility: The Steps For Coming Out On Top.

Some work environment can be hostile, or outrightly toxic. What can we do if we find ourselves in such work environment. Regardless of the cause of the hostility, there are some things we can do to thrive in such environment. This book provides an invaluable guide to success in hostile work environment.

Unplugged: Navigating The Social Media Minefield And Reclaiming Your Productivity

In this book, we embark on a journey to explore the profound impact of social media on our lives and discover practical strategies to rise above the noise and reclaim control of our time and attention.

As we navigate the digital landscape, we have unwittingly fallen into a pattern of constant connectivity—an incessant checking of notifications, scrolling through endless feeds, and succumbing to the fear of missing out (FOMO). The more we delve into the virtual world, the more we risk losing sight of our real-world aspirations and dreams.